Collective Societal Wisdom

The Centerpiece to the Longevity of Civilization

Max Parrella

Cover art by Samantha Cossen

Table of Contents

Collective Societal Wisdom

The Centerpiece to the Longevity of Civilization

Introduction

Our world has seen a number of significant events over the past few years that could have long-lasting effects on the future generations. Unfortunately, many of these events have been unsettling rather than inspiring. We have seen the rise in popularity of authoritarian figures and the growth in separatist and isolationist parties. The swiftly mounting trend of the "Us verse Them" mentality has created almost unprecedented divisiveness, even within the same communities. Because of this, countless people have had their hopes of the future shaken over the past couple years. Whether each individual's reasons for concern are geopolitical, financial, social, or something entirely different, educated people have been searching for answers as to why all these disconcerting events have been happening in the world which so many of us call "modern."

The goal of this book is to provide some insight as to why our society, and the world in general, has been flirting with a multitude of paths that could potentially be dangerous, or seemingly irrational, on a macrosociological level. Furthermore, I hope to provide some potential answers to these questions and solutions to some issues that could prevent us from going down a path of deterioration and keep us all progressing as a society and as fellow humans.

We are at an extraordinarily important point in time and our decisions, all of which affect the future in a variety of ways, must be carefully planned and executed to ensure the best possible outcomes for all of us. The world has reached a crossroads which can either take the world back to a pre-WWII isolationist state or take the world into a new era of connectivity and cooperation that has never before been seen.

Societies around the globe, with the financial crisis of 2008 still fresh in the minds of their citizens, have been struck by the yearning for new leadership as well as the temptation of isolationist nationalism in which a society feels the need to cut many of its ties with the rest of the world. This is due to the assumption that they will be able to escape the rest of the world's problems by simply not being connected to the rest of the world. In other words, this is the equivalent of the idea that if you close your eyes and cover your ears, your external problems will disappear. However, this is happening on an international scale. We have seen this recently with a number of nations electing leadership that promotes isolationist policies and there have even been outright isolationist movements such as the Brexit referendum.

The last time the world saw a situation similar to the one of current times was in the 1930's, directly in the aftermath of the Great Depression. Communities of people began to blame other communities for allegedly causing their struggles. Eventually, leadership arose claiming that it was not simply one's neighbors who caused such a crisis, but foreign communities. These leaders utilized their citizens' fear and need for answers to direct their anger and frustration at "outsiders," thus granting the leaders more power. As people became more aware of the fears outlined by these leaders, whether real or not, they became increasingly vulnerable to misinformation due to their loss of connection to the rest of the world, and thus reality, and became willing to support actions that, to one who was not wrapped up in all the chaos, were completely irrational and even immoral.

We all know the course of events from that point on, which ultimately culminated in the outbreak of WWII. Of course, I am by no means claiming that another world war is upon us or anything of the sort, but when current events begin to look like events of the past, it becomes essential to analyze the similarities of both current and past in order to aid our planning of future action in the modern world.

Using history allows us to see what worked and what did not for those who previously ran into a similar situation. Taking action without proper analysis of its potential effects can have long-lasting consequences as seen throughout history. Therefore, we must proceed with caution, but also hope, in the sense that there is always a path of progress and improvement no matter the current situation – the challenging part is to find that path and maintain that path as a common goal of humanity.

This book will further explain the importance of interconnectivity on the macro level but will also go into detail on how individual identities shape the macro scale. This book will discuss the overwhelming growth of what I call, the "Culture of Me," the trend towards individualism, and thus division within and between communities, over the last few decades.

This abundance of individualistic thinking is visible in a variety of ways in current society such as the overwhelming use of social media, where individuals want to document everything about themselves to the whole world, and other seemingly trivial trends such as the "selfie." The fleeting notion that one would rather take a photo of himself or herself is immensely different than the past where one would want to appreciate an image outside of himself or herself.

The growing perception that one's self-identity is more important than the communal identity has also resulted in the decline in group participation in the United States, with the exception of self-help groups (which ironically are about the well-being of the individual rather than the group as a whole) as well as the rise in movements that center around individual identity. These types of movements, which may seem honorable and just, can in fact be extraordinarily divisive and exclusive. These movements have become the face of the "Culture of Me." Many of these movements show how entire populations have changed their ways of thinking over the last couple generations from "How can I be more accepting of others," to "How can others be more accepting of me." Although subtle, this is an astounding shift in collective thought.

This change in thought process has grown with such force and has begun the dangerous trend of purposeful victimization. When one is constantly thinking of how mainstream society can accept them in the short term, they will surely be disappointed and angered because everybody is passionate about a different aspect of identity making it impossible for individuals to always feel accepted for all aspects of their identity by all of society. This dissonance is almost impossible to reconcile on a societal level. Sadly, if everyone could only revert back to the thought of "How can I be more accepting of others," they might find that the world becomes more open-minded much more effectively and populations may begin to find a sense of community rather than the small, divisive cohorts that aim to blame others for their struggles rather than looking inward.

Throughout this book, there will be a number of comparisons to past historical situations that can provide important insight to the causes of our current global issues which can then help us in finding proper solutions that are effective, secure, and long-lasting. The main focus of this book will be to explain the notion of what I call "Collective Societal Wisdom" and its vital importance to any and every society. This runs alongside my theory that macrosociological units such as entire civilizations have the same motives and thus actions that the smallest societal unit, the individual and his or her family, do. Throughout my analysis, reflected in the rest of this book, I have determined that the loss of interconnectivity among people, combined with the stifling of creativity, can lead to decreasing Collective Societal Wisdom amongst the citizens of a society, which can take an entire society into a backwards progression that could even bring about another Dark Age.

The Dark Ages is well known to the general public as a time of mass death and war and all the worst parts of society, however, that is not what was most significant about the Dark Ages. The single most important aspect of the Dark Ages was the loss of information, knowledge, technology, and most importantly, the shared goal of all of humanity to improve the lives of the next generation, *for everyone*. In fact, the Dark Ages is actually called the Dark Ages due to the lack of information modern historians have about it. Very few people during that time were writing things down or doing any sort of preservation or innovation for future generations for that matter. The Dark Ages was characterized by individuals simply trying to survive.

Therefore, this same definition can be used for any period of time during which the common man can do nothing else except what is immediately necessary to survive, whether that survival is in a literal sense, a financial sense, a social sense, or any other aspect of life. The Dark Ages was not dark simply because a number of Medieval knights were killing each other, it was dark because the societies of the time did not have the capacity to allow for communal progress. The sole focus was the survival of the smallest societal unit, the individual and his family. The cause of these dark times was rooted in the collapse of the greatest political, financial, and social system of the era, the Roman Empire. Later I will describe in detail the invisible causes of the Roman collapse and how it swiftly dragged the world into the Dark Ages as well as how we can prevent a similar fate in the modern world, beginning with the greatest political, financial, and social system of our era, the United States of America.

It is important to note that although much of the content described in this book can be interpreted as dark or scary, this book is not meant to fearmonger. In fact, I have a sincerely optimistic faith in humans' ability to adapt to, as well as stimulate, change. This book is meant to enlighten its readers on sociological issues that, in many cases, have their causes rooted in forces that are invisible to the general population. The first step to progress is the awareness of current issues and the hope that they are possible to change.

This book is meant to make comparisons to past situations that can help us avoid making the same mistakes again. I hope to outline these problems and their causes in an effective and understandable way to spread awareness of these invisible forces at work in anticipation that the readers will be able to help find the best path to keep our society progressing. I have presented my own opinion on what I believe the solution to be in its most general form, but ultimately, I hope the readers of this book will provide a stronger one.

As for a quick summary of myself, I am a graduate from the University of Iowa, with a degree in the studies of ancient civilizations and am currently enrolled in a Master's program in Social Work. As a millennial, I hope my message resonates with other millennials since the future of the world is literally in our hands. At this moment, our generation has the most capacity to change the world for the better if only we had the knowledge and courage needed to do so. This book aims to provide a small piece of that knowledge using comparative analysis combined with my historical background. Studying history, I have seen the successes and mistakes of countless individuals and entire civilizations, some leading to lasting prosperity and others bringing about massive collapse.

Many people have the preconceived notion that humans hundreds or thousands of years before us were somehow different than we are today – almost alien in a sense. However, people back then had the same brains as we have today with the same intelligence, values, social requirements, and even sense of humor. Therefore, the communities that these individuals made up were also of similar nature to our societies today. Does a child truly learn how hot a stove can be by their parent telling them? Or do they learn better by touching the burning hot pan? All animals, including humans, do well with guidance, but they truly learn best by their own experience.

Because societies are made up of humans, societies as entire units should learn from the experience of societies in the past as well. Since there is no better way to learn than from experience, and history is the experience of every man, woman, child, community, and civilization before us, we can use this wisdom to look at how to improve our own collective societal wisdom to maintain a path of further development in our world today.

History is also vastly important for another reason: to measure when a society is progressing or regressing. When we do not look at how our society, or other similar societies, have performed in the past, it becomes impossible to know when we are moving forwards or backwards.

This book will talk about how, in much of the developed world, many aspects of society seem to be regressing when compared with procedures used to measure societal advancement. Even some of the most basic aspects of civilization seem to be in jeopardy. For example, the peak, and some even argue decline, of language use in the Western World. Thousands of years ago written language developed from pictures, to glyphs, then to syllabaries, and finally alphabets. However, with the overwhelming influence of social media and instant messaging, the developed world seems to be communicating more and more through pictures and glyphs, which come in the form of memes and emoticons, rather than structured written language. This represents a decline in verbal and written language skills, ultimately showing a regression in communication, interconnectivity and societal advancement.

Because I have lived within, and extensively studied Western civilization, particularly the United States, this book will focus mainly on the issues surrounding these nations, although much of the ideologies discussed are shared by all humans and can thus be applied to any society around the world. I cannot stress enough that the purpose of this book is not only to get people thinking, but to educate those who may not know how the macrosystems in place affect them, in the hope that it will inspire those people to strive for change.

Finally, this book will discuss how significant the wealth gap in the US truly is and how this affects not only the lower classes but the upper classes as well. In 2017, the Institute for Policy Studies published a study showing that the three richest Americans, Jeff Bezos, Bill Gates, and Warren Buffet, hold more wealth than the entire bottom 50% of Americans combined. That's right. Three men hold more wealth than the collective wealth of over 160 million Americans. Luckily, these men give vast amounts to charity and support many wonderful causes but the wealth gap in the United States has become too significant to ignore. The same study further explains that one in five households in America hold a zero or negative net worth. Although it is easy to explain how these drastic figures affect the bottom 50%, I will explain how dramatic income inequality can affect every member of society, even the wealthy.

Because some powerful families try with all their might to keep the majority of us in the dark when it comes to these deliberate, systemic attacks on the working-class, the majority of Americans are unaware as to how unfair the system really is or even how much wealthier the "wealthy" really are. I hope that this book can reach those people and enlighten them so that they know who they are working for, and who they should be working with, ultimately so that we all can join together and stimulate much-needed reform in the United States. Of course, money is not inherently bad, but the ways in which it is manipulated by some in the US deems a closer look.

There is one more thing I would like to disclose about this book. This book is not designed for the academics. This book is not put together with decades of large, corporate-funded research projects. Rather, this book is a journal of thoughts and theories by one man who hopes to start a conversation. This book is meant to be a quick and easy read highlighting the strengths and weaknesses of modern society and how we can preserve progress. I ultimately hope that these ideas, combined with thousands of years of societal experience, in other words, history, can stimulate ideas and actions that may otherwise be left static. Welcome to *Collective Societal Wisdom: The Centerpiece to the Longevity of Civilization.*

PART I

The Inner Workings of Collective Societal Wisdom and How CSW Affects Societies

Collective Societal Wisdom

As stated earlier, the loss of interconnectivity among people leads to decreasing Collective Societal Wisdom, which is a defining factor of any society of all levels. Collective Societal Wisdom (Which I will consequently refer to as "CSW") is the most important measure which can identify the capacity of a society to advance. So, before explaining anything further, what exactly is Collective Societal Wisdom?

CSW is a measure of the following:

I. *The overall learned knowledge of an entire society at the present time*

II. *A society's collective ability to analyze and utilize previous knowledge and diverse perspectives to build upon, improve, and create new knowledge*

III.   *The knowledge and understanding of a society's average citizen about the workings of societal institutions, current and past events, and ideologies, and how that knowledge impacts the citizen's capacity to think in terms of bettering the future for himself and those around him.*

IV.   *The level of motivation to improve society regarding a variety of aspects including financial, moral, social, legal, technological, educational etc.*

V.   *And finally, the society's actual ability to maximize its output of resources, both physical such as money and intangible such as influence, as well as the previously stated factors, to use for the ultimate cause - to advance the well-being of humanity*

To give a better understanding, I will provide details and real-world examples for each of the factors contributing to CSW.

I.   *The overall learned knowledge of an entire society at the present time:*

For anyone or any community to function, they must simply learn things and preserve the knowledge. Of course, different communities around the world can have drastically different levels of knowledge. Since new knowledge can only be created using previously learned knowledge, the more knowledge a nation has access to allows for greater opportunity for the creation of new knowledge.

The first factor in determining a society's Collective Societal Wisdom is the actual base of knowledge that they already have at the present time. It is extremely difficult for societies to significantly advance if they simply have a lesser base of knowledge and experience. The same difficulties arise if a society has misinformed or outdated knowledge. The most important aspect that contributes to a society's base knowledge is the nature of preserving the things that one learns or experiences for future generations. Imagine if a great thinker such as Isaac Newton or Einstein had not passed on their knowledge to anybody. It would have taken much longer for people to come to the same conclusions and be able to frame it in a way that makes sense.

In fact, many of the most famous innovators were able to achieve greatness by finishing the uncompleted work of others. Some famous examples include Thomas Edison and the lightbulb, Galileo and the telescope, and Guglielmo Marconi and the radio. Without their base knowledge, it would have been impossible for them to achieve the same level of advancement.

However, it is also important to note that this overall learned knowledge cannot only be shared by a few people. The knowledge and experience must be spread across the majority of the population for it to be most effective. There are two reasons for this: the first and most obvious is that more knowledge and experience can help people become more successful, more efficient, and achieve a larger capacity to learn and preserve even more information. The second reason is for innovative purposes. Everybody knows two heads is better than one. But when one increases this by many order of magnitudes, massive success can be achieved.

Statistically, more people who know more things will provide greater innovation by the sheer increase in the number of people who may be trying to innovate, preserve, or create. If there is a problem and only one person knows about it, the solution will take tremendously longer to find. However, if there are many people from different backgrounds and with different perspectives who know about the problem, odds are a variety of solutions will present themselves and at a much quicker pace.

Overall knowledge of the general population can be measured by looking at issues in which every member of the population could be exposed to such as health problems. Everyone has a body and therefore one's knowledge of health can be an important marker of the level of knowledge the majority of a society has on the most basic level.

For example, we can use two drastically different examples of the AIDS epidemic to show both the importance of this first tier of CSW as well as how to measure it. The first I would like to discuss is the AIDS issue as seen in many parts of Africa, particularly the southeast. As many already know, these parts of Africa have the most heavily infected HIV populations in the world with over half of all people living with HIV in the world residing in these areas (Avert, 2019). Despite the terrifying statistics of this region, the epidemic is in fact declining. In 2016, UNAIDS reported that over 76% of people living with HIV are aware of their disease and 79% of those people are receiving treatment. Consequently, the number of new cases of HIV is declining in the same region.

This is due to the incredible education programs within the region. In the beginning of the epidemic, when AIDS was first recognized, the disease spread so fast because these populations simply did not know what the disease was or how it was spread. The lack of a basic education for living a healthy lifestyle allowed the disease to turn into an epidemic of massive scale. However, through years of educating the population, results are finally starting to show, and new cases are declining every year.

To reiterate, the lack of adequate education which gave rise to a lack of basic knowledge about healthcare turned the AIDS epidemic in Africa into one of the worst human tragedies in history. Luckily, as we have seen in Africa, increasing education can solve the problem. Of course, the AIDS epidemic in Africa is not news for any of us in the western world thanks to strong programs spreading awareness. It is easy to forget that developed nations can also be affected by a lack of basic knowledge, even regarding healthcare issues such as HIV.

In fact, the only place in the world where the number of new AIDS cases is actually rising happens to be in the developed world. Russia, and some other parts of eastern Europe, has a rate of HIV infections growing by 10-15% each year and 1% of the current adult population has been estimated to already be infected. In only the last 10 years in Russia, the number of newly diagnosed people with AIDS has increased 149%. These numbers are catastrophic for any society.

What is even more interesting, however, is the fact that Russia boasts a socialized healthcare system with extensive infrastructure. With regards to resources, Russia enjoyed an average of 4.0 physicians per 1000 people and 8.1 hospital beds per 1000 people in 2017 which was much higher than the average for developed nations. This compares to 2.6 physicians per 1000 people and 2.8 hospital beds per 1000 people in the United States (OECD, 2017). So why then is there a massive increase in the number of HIV cases in Russia when HIV is generally extremely well known in developed healthcare systems.

As I am sure you expected, the cause is rooted in the first tier of CSW, overall learned knowledge *of an entire society*. This last part is the most important factor with regards to the AIDS epidemic in Russia. Although the Russian government, in coordination with health experts, has collected widespread evidence of the AIDS epidemic and its causes, the government refuses to acknowledge that AIDS is a real threat and therefore does not inform the general population, or anybody for that matter, about its causes, symptoms, or prevention.

As explained earlier, if only a small portion of the population knows something, it is as if that knowledge does not exist at all. Using Russia and southern and eastern Africa as examples, it becomes clear that societies cannot advance, and can even regress as is happening in Russia, if knowledge and experience is not shared with the general population.

II.   *A society's collective ability to analyze and utilize previous knowledge and perspectives to build upon, improve, and create new knowledge:*

The second tier of Collective Societal Wisdom is a society's capacity to use old knowledge to create new knowledge. This is what many call the process of innovation. In the last two decades, innovation has become a widely used term in developed nations, particularly in the world of business. With the onset of the "startup," every business promotes their product or service as innovative and progressive in order to market themselves as a contemporary company. However, despite innovation becoming a popular catchphrase in the corporate business sector, which of course encompasses the vast majority of products and services provided to developed nations, an exceptionally large number of people do not actually seem to know what it means to truly innovate.

True innovation comes when old knowledge, perspectives, and ideas are analyzed and combined with other knowledge, perspectives, and ideas to create something completely new, in the form of either an idea, a technology, a product, a policy, a perspective, or even an action. Everything new is built from the mixing and matching of knowledge, ideas, or perspectives that already exist.

Thus, the second tier of CSW can be defined as a society's adaptability to the constantly-changing world combined with its actual capacity to innovate. It is important to note that innovation comes in the form of extensive analysis (this is widely known as "research") of knowledge and technologies across multiple fields as well as the blending of multiple perspectives. With this in mind, we can assume that a society's second tier CSW, or its capacity to innovate as well as adapt to others' innovations, can be measured by the amount of freedom its population possesses to interact intelligently with those of differing disciplines and perspectives.

In other words, a society which does not allow the easy transfer of technology and ideas across varying disciplines finds itself innovating at a much slower, expensive, and laborious rate than a society which encourages interdisciplinary interactions and studies.

For those who prefer numerical measurements, a strong statistic to look at describing a nation's innovation is the number of patents issued per year. One can look at the trend of the number of patents filed to look at how many technologies are granted as new and then compare this to other nations.

For example, the US and China are extremely different societies in numerous ways. But most importantly, the US is extremely individualistic and has been becoming increasingly isolated. Even within the US, different fields are becoming more and more isolated from other fields of study.

This is vastly different than China due to significant cultural differences. China is largely communal. The majority of people in China, and other East-Asian societies, put the priorities of the community as a whole over those of the individual. On the largest scale, this means the priorities and well-being of China as a whole is more important than that of the individual. Over the last fifteen years, China has increased certain freedoms allowing researchers and businesses to work together much easier. This interdisciplinary freedom, combined with the communal-centric attitudes of the Chinese people has become a formidable innovative power, especially compared to the US, which for almost all its history has been known as the most innovative place in the world.

Let's look at the numbers. In 2004, the United States had roughly 189,000 patent applications from those who resided in the US and 167,000 patent applications from non-residents. This compares to 65,000 resident applications and 64,000 non-resident applications for patents in China in the same year. Each nation has slightly more resident applications than non-resident although the ratio is about half and half. It is also important to note that the US clearly had a significant innovative edge over China due to the sheer number of patent applications in the US compared to China. However, this changes drastically only ten years later.

In 2014, after some important reforms in China allowing greater access to outside technology and information, China's patents have skyrocketed.

The US in 2014 boasted 285,000 resident patent applications and 293,000 non-resident applications. This is interesting because there are now much more foreign applications being filed in the US than actual US residents compared to 2004.

China however shows a completely different story. China's resident applications in 2014 were over 800,000. Yes, 800,000 – more than all of the US patents combined. Furthermore, China's non-resident patent apps only reached a mere 127,000 (Jones, 2016).

Looking at these numbers, it becomes clear that the amount of new technology coming out of China is growing at an exceptional rate, even compared to the United States, or the "Capital of Innovation," whose ratio of domestic to foreign patent applications is actually decreasing. Although patent statistics are only one tiny portion of what makes up the second tier of Collective Societal Wisdom, statistics such as these provide important numerical data which make it easy to analyze trends and compare to other areas of business, or even entire nations.

In short, China's new policies of openness to new ideas and new connections has led to an incredible explosion in innovation while the growing culture of individualism in the United States has led to innovative stagnation for those who actually reside in the US.

Regardless, much of CSW is difficult to measure numerically, and the second tier is no different. Unfortunately, the western world generally only measures importance in numbers and thus when something lacks strong numerical data, it becomes considered unimportant and is tossed aside. This type of attitude is so deeply embedded in American culture in particular that it even delves into American education systems and policy. For example, areas of study that cannot be measured by a test score, in other words fields that are based around creativity such as the liberal arts, are not only underfunded but are even looked down upon by those who belong to fields in which everything can be measured and compared in numbers.

I will explain the consequences of a society only centered around numerical data in later chapters but, before I continue, I find it exceptionally important to stress that there is much more to the world than statistics, plots, and other numerical data. And furthermore, simply because a certain theory, method of action, or field of study is not backed by numerical measurement absolutely does not make it irrelevant or any less important than those that can be easily quantified.

As for the second tier of CSW, comparisons cannot always be made by plain numbers. It is much too complicated a measurement to try to use only numerical value-holders to quantify and compare a society's overall ability to analyze and use previous knowledge and various perspectives to build upon, improve, and create new knowledge and perspectives. However, as one begins to understand the different aspects of Collective Societal Wisdom, it becomes easier and easier to see it within different aspects of society, even when one is not looking for it.

III.   *The knowledge and understanding of a society's average citizen about the workings of societal institutions, current and past events, and ideologies, and how that knowledge impacts the citizen's capacity to think in terms of bettering the future for himself and those around him:*

The third tier of Collective Societal Wisdom can be defined as a population's level of understanding of the actual workings of society and how these events, institutions, or beliefs affect the many aspects of that society as well as other societies. Furthermore, one must understand the workings of other societies to better comprehend the effects that society has on one's own population.

For example, the United States currently has the most powerful and influential economic system in the world. The news is filled with articles on the actions of various businesses, and universities are filled with students studying business or finance or economics. However, almost nobody within the US actually understands how the American financial system functions. Capitalism is the term that is thrown around left and right to define the American financial powerhouse but how many people actually know what capitalism is, or what its implications are for the general population?

Does the average American know that capitalism requires a certain number of people to always be in debt? Does the average American know that the rate of unemployment is manipulated to always keep a certain percentage of "healthy" unemployment to allow room for economic growth? Ask any American if they know that the Federal Reserve, which is not actually government-owned but is a private entity, manipulates interest rates to keep inflation rising, and thus the value of your money falling, so that the actual value of the US debt continues to fall and more debt, and thus capital, becomes cheaper and cheaper to issue[3] (See Further Readings). If you ask most Americans questions such as these, which are vital to understanding the American financial system, the odds are they have no idea about any of these things.

Most ordinary civilians in any developed nation take a whole lot of systems in place for granted, both good and bad. This usually comes in some form of statements such as, "Well, that's just the way it is," or "It's always been that way." Unfortunately, these are not reasons for accepting "the way things are" but rather catchphrases designed to keep all of us ordinary citizens from questioning these systems. Take the right to vote. How many ordinary Americans have questioned why election day in the US is on a Tuesday? Has anyone wondered why the right to vote for government officials, one of the most powerful freedoms in the world, has been placed on a day where the vast majority of people work in the US?

There are many theories regarding why Tuesday was first set as the election day, many involving religion and the agrarian nature of society back in the day, however, the law has not been adapted to meet a modernized nation. Why is this? Why could election day not be moved to sometime over the weekend like a Saturday? It seems that for some elitist parties, the Tuesday election day actually works out quite nicely.

It seems that a number of influential members of the rich, powerful, and elite members of society greatly fear losing their power and status. Many elite members of society do not want to share their wealth or power with the lower classes. However, due to the democratic nature of the US, the working class could potentially vote representatives into government who could tax the wealthy more, regulate businesses more strictly, increase minimum wage, and improve other areas of society that create overwhelming wealth gaps. But the question becomes: how do the elites prevent this from happening, especially since there are tens of millions more working-class Americans than there are rich and powerful citizens.

Well, the obvious answer is to limit the votes. And the easiest way to limit the votes of the working class is to keep election day on a day where the working class is working. This hugely limits the votes of the working class, as many of them do not have time to vote due to their commute or the hours of their jobs. Many of the middle and lower classes have kids to take care of before and after work and simply cannot afford to miss time at work or at home in order to vote.

Conservatives like to use the excuse that this population could do early-voting (in the 37 states that allow early voting) or send in an absentee ballot (in the 27 states that allow excuse-free absentee ballot), but the truth is that many working-class Americans don't know about these alternate ways to vote, and even if they do, they may not know what resources to use so they can understand how to use them.

Understanding societal institutions such as economic or civil systems, or even social constructs which may not actually be tangible institutions but still exist nonetheless (such as the attitudes of certain portions of the population or common trends among different populations), as well as understanding how certain events can impact these institutions, is vital to a population's CSW.

IV. *The level of motivation to improve society regarding a variety of aspects including financial, moral, social, legal, technological, educational etc.*

This piece of Collective Societal Wisdom has to do with the drive for progress among a population. The previous three parts of CSW regard the actual capacity of learning within a general population; however, this piece is the measurement of that population's mindset.

In every nation in the world, the population can be split into two groups. The first group, which is usually the majority of the population, can be called, the B Group. The B Group holds all the people in a society whose lives are defined by just "getting by." An overwhelming portion of these people are usually in survival-mode. All of their time and effort is rooted in simply surviving, and in most cases, helping their family survive.

Because the members of the B Group must utilize all their time, effort, money, influence, and brainpower to survive, they are rarely able to participate in helping the nation as a whole advance. When an individual and his or her family are living paycheck to paycheck, struggling to put food on the table, or stressing about financial or physical security, he or she understandably cannot focus on the progress of the nation. This means that the B Group is an untapped resource. There are millions of people within the B Group who are not any less intelligent than those outside of the B Group, but due to the stresses that affect them individually, they are not able to put their efforts towards helping the nation. To put it into the nicest terms possible, this is extraordinarily inefficient for any nation.

Before discussing the A Group, I find it important to note that there is also another subgroup within the B Group besides those who are in survival-mode. This group can be called the Bb Group. The Bb Group has access to resources and may even hold some sort of influence. These people are generally successful enough to have some free time on the weekends and also have a chunk of discretionary spending money. However, this population is completely satisfied with how things are going. They are content, they are not constantly stressing, and they can enjoy themselves with what they have. Essentially, they are so comfortable with how things are at present, that they have lost the drive to create change.

This mindset is usually visible not only in regard to creating change on a macro-scale, but also becomes visible in the personal life of that individual as well. These people are usually very passive. They may say they will do this new thing, or start that new project, but then over time they just "never got around to it."

Just like the other side of the B Group, the Bb Group too is an untapped resource for societal progress. By being passive in their individual lives, the Bb Group members learn to accept "the way things are" in both their own lives and society in general. Like the previous B Group, the Bb Group are not any less intelligent than the rest of society, but their brainpower and resources and influence are not participating in the advancement of society.

Contrary to the B Group, as you may have guessed, there is what I call the A Group. The A Group is action-oriented. These are the people who possess a strong drive to create change in society and advance the human race as a whole. Unfortunately, the A Group is usually a tiny minority in the greater population, but they still manage to make significant advances and generally hold widespread influence among their society.

Before moving forward, I would like to note that the A Group is not to be confused with the rich and powerful. In fact, the majority of the A Group are middle class. This difference is important to distinguish because many Westerners see the upper class pouring money into charities or political parties and so on. However, this does not make them a part of the A Group. The wealthy members of society who put millions of dollars into charities solely for tax cuts are not members of the A Group. The wealthy and powerful members of society who spend massive amounts of time and resources to influence politics for personal interest are also not a part of the A Group. These people are still a part of the Bb Group because, although they may have a drive for change that affects them personally, they do not have a drive to advance all of society for all its members.

The focus of the A group resides in universal progress: That is, progress that encompasses every human within every society. The true members of the A group not only donate money but donate their minds. The A Group maintains an unwavering focus on full societal progress and will stop at nothing to achieve that. We can applaud the A Group for their efforts this far; however, greater advancement will come with greater connections and greater knowledge.

Thus, we can challenge the A Group to work together in determining solutions with the following purpose: To bring as many B Group and Bb group members over into the A Group as possible. Although both A and B groups are different than one another, they are always fluid. And just as B Group members can join the A Group, A Group members must be sure to take care of other A Group members to ensure they do not lose focus or give up and fall into the Bb Group.

With regards to Collective Societal Wisdom, the greater the ratio of minds within A Group to that of those in B Group, the faster and more significant will the advancement of their society be.

V.   *Society's actual ability to maximize its output of resources, both physical such as money and intangible such as influence, as well as the previously stated factors, to use for the ultimate cause - to advance the well-being of humanity*

This final piece of Collective Societal Wisdom defines the fluidity of the previous four factors in coming together for the ultimate goal – advancing the welfare of humanity. The question of this final piece is as such: To what extent is the society using the previous factors of CSW to create macro-scale action in a direction that promotes global progress?

For instance, a society which appears to have high levels of tangible and intellectual resources but lacks motivation for change or lacks a sense of communal identity outside of the individual or family unit, does not have a high level of CSW despite the fact that measurables such as literacy rates may allude to the fact that the population may be "educated."

Everybody probably knew that one individual who had huge potential and was provided with an abundance of resources and support but fails to utilize them efficiently, or at all, and thus fell into a life of stagnation, or in some cases, regression. The same principle applies to entire societies.

The Social Values Spectrum

Every society in the world has some type of constitution, code of laws, set of traditions, unwritten moral codes, and probably a mix of the above. Many of us know this and take it for granted. However, just as large communities or movements have codes that help them make decisions, every individual has a code as well. Although one's code may not be written out in constitutional lingo, each individual's actions generally reflect his or her code.

These codes usually arise without any sort of deliberate thinking. Nobody sits down when he or she becomes an adult and states, "Well it's time I make a code to help me make decisions in the future." No, these codes are formed implicitly by teachings, experiences, upbringing, and of course agreement or disagreement with the codes of their society. Likewise, many of us non-philosophers do not come to a decision and think, "Wait, let me check my code before I make a decision," but rather the decision is already sent through the code in the unconscious brain and a decision is made.

I would argue that the vast majority of decisions we make on a daily basis are unconscious, even though they may feel like we are actually deciding. In fact, most decisions are probably already decided before they even make it to our conscious mind – essentially our brain already knows what action it will take before we are even aware that this decision is present. These actions are known as habit loops[4] (See Further Readings).

So how does any of this have to do with macro-level action? Well, if the majority of individual decision-making is determined unconsciously through a code which the individual may be largely unaware of, and if human actions are determined by these unconscious decisions, one can assume that these actions are made unconsciously, but are determined by this code at the heart of every individual.

Although each individual has a specific code, there is one aspect which is at the heart of the code of every individual. This aspect is evolutionary by purpose, but can cause issues when it comes to the well-being of a group versus the well-being of an individual: Every code of every individual, unless it is interfered with, naturally puts the number one priority without exception as maintaining and/or forwarding the well-being of oneself and one's family or inner circle.

The family unit has the strongest bond of any group because each family unit is bound by the most powerful force in the universe, love. At times societies as a whole can act as a family unit in which their macro-level actions reflect the yearning to improve its well-being. However, societies are not bound by love but are bound by the yearning for collective gains for every family unit within. This slight difference between the goal of the family unit and that of the societal unit is a disjuncture where problems arise.

This disjuncture is where social values come into play. Many already understand the nature of social values and take them for granted. Social values are the unwritten codes of large groups of people within a culture. There are essentially infinite possible combinations of social values within one single society, let alone the entire world. However, all social values can be placed on a line, which I will call the Social Value Spectrum, or SVS. The SVS can help us determine the general consensus of the population regarding what actions to take when, and can thus predict future actions of an entire society.

So, what is the common factor among all social values that can allows us to place them on a line? The Social Value Spectrum defines the balance, or imbalance, of a society's prioritization of action between helping oneself or one's own family unit, and helping every other family units within the society.

For example, a capitalistic society with a significant portion of the population that believes in minimal social welfare policies would tip the SVS scale towards prioritizing the single-family unit. This is because those who believe in cutting social welfare policies would rather have less taxes for him or herself and his or her family than setting up safety nets to catch other families who are struggling.

On the other hand, a society with a large portion of the population that believes in universal healthcare, subsidized child day-care, or other similar beliefs, will tip the scale towards the prioritization of the greater well-being.

Depending on which side of the Social Values Spectrum the majority of people are, or at least a majority of the people in power are, one can predict the actions of entire societies and can also understand past actions of those societies. The overall CSW of a society will directly impact that society's social values and on which side of the spectrum they reside.

A wonderful study in a powerful nation such as the United States would be to survey as much of the population as is feasible to determine their social values. Each common social value as determined by the researcher would be a category under which people could identify or not. More people within a certain value would give that point a greater magnitude. Then these points could be plotted on a visual version of the Social Values Spectrum to quantify the mindsets and social values of an entire nation. This could be used as an index to measure nations, corporations, or any such group where the goals of the individuals may clash with the goal of the common good.

One example of the goals of individuals potentially risking the well-being of the society is the hyper-individualistic nature of Western civilization that has hugely grown in recent history. I describe this new trend in thought the "Culture of Me."

The "Culture of Me"

Highly developed societies around the world have become increasingly individualistic in nature, so much so that deliberately promoting one's identity externally has become the accepted standard in these cultures. In fact, entire movements dedicated to externalizing individual identity have become extremely active as well. This is not to say that many of these movements are not rooted in moral causes, and this is certainly not saying that distinguishing one's own identity is unimportant, but the phenomenon of all these movements exploding in membership over the last decade or two is noteworthy on a societal level and the cause should be examined.

The prevalence of this individualistic thought process can be seen most easily by the explosion of something incredibly simple: the "selfie." The idea of taking a picture of oneself, and then sharing it with as many people as possible, is an exceptionally individualistic thought process. The shift in thought from "How can I appreciate others," to "How can others appreciate me" reveals a striking change in the values of modern culture.

This individualistic shift in thought process on a societal level can further be seen by the numerous movements centered around individual identity. Despite the wonderful efforts made to increase awareness of various communities and showcase their struggles with being part of a minority population within the greater society, these movements further reveal a swift shift in thought process from the desire to care for the entire society to the care of the individual, or at least a small group of like-minded individuals (similar to a family unit as described earlier).

There are two such changes in societal thought, particularly in the Western world that have occurred quite quickly. The first has been a change from, "How can I be more accepting to those around me" to "How can those around me be more accepting of me." The second change has been from "How can I, and those similar to me, take care of those who are different from me" to "How can those who are different from me take care of me and those similar to me."

The contrast between thinking inward about one's actions towards others and thinking externally about the actions of society towards the individual is striking. Movements of the latter type must take great care in how they are managed because, in some cases, movements trying to establish societal action to aid a vulnerable group can actually make the situation, and people involved, more divisive.

This contrast in thoughts and actions is almost identical to the contrast between the civil rights movements of Martin Luther King Jr. and Malcolm X. Martin Luther King Jr. expressed the importance of respectful, all-inclusive, non-aggressive protest. On the contrary, Malcolm X expressed that the pride and identity of his people was most important. Furthermore, he wanted this pride and identity to be externalized. Malcolm X wanted his people to "defend themselves" against the white suppression.

He even criticized Martin Luther King Jr. in the words, "The white man pays Reverend Martin Luther King, subsidizes Reverend Martin Luther King, so that Reverend Martin Luther King can continue to teach the negroes to be defenseless. That's what you mean by non-violent: be defenseless. Be defenseless in the face of one of the most cruel beasts that has ever taken a people into captivity. That's just the American white man" (Baldwin, 1986).

Interestingly, many of the active movements in the current time are taking after the external pride-based style of Malcolm X, rather than an all-inclusive, universal Martin Luther King Jr. approach. The fact that topics surrounding identity are still extremely sensitive to discuss, especially with many members of these movements, shows that "defenses" are up among these groups. This, in turn, raises defenses and sensitivity in other communities as well. Unfortunately, this chain of sensitivity and defensiveness can actually render these movements to be more divisive, which is the exact opposite of the original purpose of these movements.

The entire Culture of Me has already had drastic impacts on the populations of Western society, especially the United States. The externalizing of one's identity on platforms such as social media, which has become a social norm, can be exhausting, and for many young people, hugely difficult. This is because most young people have not fully found themselves or created their own identity yet. The formation of one's identity takes time and experience.

However, with the high-speed nature of everything else in modern society, young people are quick to take shortcuts regarding their identity. Because of this, many young people take factors such as DSM disorders, gender identities, political views, or other set "identity factors," and thus form their own identity entirely around that specific factor.

A young adult or adolescent who is diagnosed with generalized anxiety or depression, for example, may take that disorder and build their complete identity around it. Whether this is a conscious decision or unconscious phenomenon does not matter. But odds are if you ask this person to tell you about him or herself, he or she would state that he has depression or anxiety as one of the first identifying factors.

Sadly, this could lead to that young adult growing up associating loneliness or sadness, or any other symptom of depression or anxiety, with his or her own identity in the long term. The same goes for the entire new Culture of Me. If the younger generations are growing up thinking about how everybody around them can help them feel more comfortable rather than how they can help those around them feel more comfortable, divisions between communities will inherently be created, or deepened. In other words, these mindsets run the risk of creating an identity bystander effect, where everybody believes the source of one's comfort is in somebody else's court. Furthermore, the fact that no single individual will find another individual with completely identical values means that if this culture continues to grow stronger, eventually everybody will be frustrated because they will be perceived to be alone since they cannot find others to accept all their values or beliefs.

Thus, although it is extremely important, and even essential, to have the freedom to present one's identity however he or she may choose, those within large identity movements must take great care in how they manage these movements so that they do not create a more divisive society, which could eventually sabotage the wonderful cause they were fighting for in the first place.

How CSW Impacts the Direction of Society

You now know what Collective Societal Wisdom actually is and some ways of measuring the various aspects of the term among societies. However, the true importance of CSW is how it effects one or more communities in the future. CSW is the single greatest driving force for the well-being of a community of people, some as small as a tribe or even a corporate team, and some as large as entire nations.

The CSW of a community directly determines what direction this community of people will take – forwards or backwards – as well as the rate of their progression or regression. What is surprising to most people is that many aspects of CSW have little correlation with the industrial/financial level of the nation. There are many advanced, powerful, rich nations that actually have populations with relatively low CSW. Some reasons for this include massive populations which make it difficult to educate all of them, but also the education itself can be to blame in many cases as well. For instance, deliberate miseducation such as in the Russian AIDS disaster will devastate a society's CSW.

In its most general terms, Collective Societal Wisdom is the measure of competency, understanding, and motivation to reach a goal that would help a *community,* not an individual, *long term.* The issue of improving a community long term is where things start to get complicated. Obviously, there are countless communities around the world with many even overlapping, and each community has different short and medium-term goals than the next. These goals can be at odds with the Universal Goal that every community shares: to make the world a better place for the next generation of that community. It is important to note that of course there are individuals around the world who do not share this universal goal, but the overwhelming majority of humanity does.

There are a few major problems that arise from this idea of improving communities long term. The first is that there is a strong correlation between CSW and goal prioritization. Low CSW generally yields a higher number of short-term goals that take priority over the long-term goals, especially the Universal Goal. This is particularly visible on the individual level with the younger generations requiring instant gratification, which affects their spending habits, mental health, and even takes them down a path of "quick fixes" to their problems, such as medicating themselves with illegal or pharmaceutical drugs. Higher levels of CSW allows greater foresight into the future and thus leads to communities prioritizing time, resources, and planning to be allocated for long-term goal achievement, including of course the Universal Goal.

Another significant problem arises when two communities or societies bump into each other while trying to achieve their short-term goals or increase their short-term well-being. This can cause arguments or suspicions over just about anything and many times they are just that, baseless arguments or suspicions. But on a larger scale, this can lead to massive crises, such as war, which almost always leads to a decrease in both societies' well-being in the long run.

This idea of shortsightedness among communities in the sense of prioritizing short-term gains while failing to see long-term results has been coined as the Tragedy of the Commons. The term "Tragedy of the Commons" was created by Garrett Hardin in 1968 to explain how individuals within a group acting selfishly for short-term gains can actually hurt the entire group including themselves as individuals. Everyone becomes worse-off than before. Today, the most widely used examples of the

Tragedy of the Commons are used in the field of environmental science.

A common example, and the one originally described by Hardin, involves a community of cattle herders who share a common grazing ground for their cattle. Let's say the grounds can support the feeding of 1000 cattle and there are 1000 farmers who each own one cow. Everything works out perfectly at this point. However, Farmer Bob comes up with the brilliant idea to buy another cow so that he now has two cattle. This instantly doubles his profits, and only takes up extra food consumption equivalent to 0.1% of the entire ground's capacity. However, other farmers see Farmer Bob raking in the cash, so they all decide to buy an extra cow. Suddenly, there are 2000 cattle on grounds only able to support 1000. Quite rapidly, the grounds become overgrazed and at the end of the year there is no food left for any of the cattle. The farmers than have two choices: either let their cattle die which would mean no income for the farmers or move to another grazing ground which would then cause overgrazing in that area due to the influx of cattle. Either way, a large number of cattle farmers are going to accrue significant losses.

This notion of the Tragedy of the Commons can be used to describe entire societies as well. A society acting only for short-term gains, whether these gains are social, financial, or political, without foresight as to what these actions may lead to in the long term, can cause drastic issues for both their own people as well as many others who are not members of their society.

The Tragedy of the Commons explains how individuals or communities acting rationally can actually diminish their own well-being, and in many cases the well-being of many others. And, this is of course assuming that these actors are thinking rationally. In many fields of study such as economics, political analysis, and game theory, the idea that all individuals act rationally to promote their own self-interests is assumed. However, as nice as that would be, that assumption does not actually apply to much of the real world. The truth of the matter is that almost the entirety of humanity are not rational actors, but rather act based on emotion.

The Tragedy of the Commons is a keen way of explaining how even rational actors or communities can actually sabotage themselves in the long term. However, the problem of self-sabotage is further exacerbated by the fact that communities are made up of human beings, and despite the common misconception that humans are rational, human beings are hugely impacted by emotional responses and thus rarely, if ever, act rationally.

This is mostly due to the fact that emotions, and the brain's response to emotions, are rooted in actual scientific molecular inputs and hormonal responses. Essentially, our emotional responses happen automatically within our unconscious mind. Furthermore, when our emotions are validated by others, we feel even better. This starkly contrasts with how our rational minds work. The rational mind is only located in our conscious mind. Only our conscious mind can use logic and reason, and uses exactly those to override our unconscious mind when we choose. Unfortunately, most people underestimate the power of the unconscious, emotional mind. And furthermore, many fail to see how one's emotional response can alter their perspective on things before the information is even presented to the conscious, rational mind.

More importantly, there are some emotions that do not go through the rational mind at all. Fear, for example, completely bypasses the rational mind and is so powerful that fear can actually make decisions and actions itself, without even consulting the conscious mind. Have you ever watched a scary movie, and screamed or jumped without ever commanding your body to do so? That reaction is not simply a muscle reaction but was commanded by your brain. However, it was not commanded by your conscious mind, but rather was an unconscious command that completely bypassed your conscious, logical mind. Even though every part of your rational mind knows that nothing is actually going to jump out of the screen, your unconscious mind can still command your body to act. This is because fear is one of the most ancient and powerful emotions. I will go into fear itself in more detail in the following chapter, but I want to stress the importance of recognizing that powerful emotional responses can alter any human's rational thinking and can even force decisions or actions by bypassing the conscious mind altogether.

It is for this reason that fearmongers can create such widespread action among large populations. If one can appeal to an entire society's fear response, that individual can convince that society of essentially anything because in the time that the individuals are in a fear-response, their conscious, rational mind will be turned off, or at least bypassed. In fact, when one is afraid, blood actually drains from the brain and enters the muscles, making parts of the brain less powerful. Going back to the scary movie example, everybody should be familiar with the feeling after being spooked. Your heart is racing, your muscles are tense, and furthermore, even though you know with 100% certainty that nothing is going to physically jump out of the screen and put you in any danger whatsoever, your unconscious mind took control and reacted by itself.

This reactionary emotional response is the same response that enabled Adolf Hitler to commandeer the minds of so many millions of people in the 1930s and 40s. By appealing to fear, the second most powerful emotion (second only to love), Hitler was able to bypass the logical thinking of millions of people and directed their emotional reactions into actions that he commanded.

In Hitler's case, he was able to convert the fear response to bring about another emotion, anger. As we all know, anger is another emotion that can swiftly bypass the rational mind and act upon its own whim. By illuminating the Germans' economic fears in the 1930s, and blaming the economic problems on the Jewish people, Hitler was able to instill such an angry reaction from large portions of the German populace that it resulted in them supporting him and seemingly blindly following his commands.

This same technique was repeated in the political spectrum in the United States during the 1950s and 1960s. In what was known as the "Southern Strategy," Republican candidates such as Barry Goldwater and Richard Nixon used the economic and social fears of the white Southerners to instill anger and indirectly blame the African Americans so that the white Southerners would unconsciously identify with these candidates, eventually casting their votes for them.

As horrible as it was, "Coded Racism" as it was called, was hugely successful, again due to its appeal to the irrational, emotional, unconscious mind which prompted action without the checks and balances of the logical, conscious mind.

All of this means that just as individuals can largely act irrationally, and are activated by irrational thinking, entire communities or societies will act irrationally as well. Without any rational thinking, societies can quickly begin to lose focus on long-term implications of short-term actions the same way an individual might be angry and hit somebody without thinking of the long-term implications.

Of course, sometimes an emotional response can be helpful as it can aid in understanding others and building relationships. But we must still take care to utilize logic and insight into how our actions will affect ourselves and others over the long term.

High levels of Collective Societal Wisdom will counteract this emotional thinking and bring back some logic and reason, especially regarding long-lasting impacts of actions on the future. In other words, as Collective Societal Wisdom declines, so does understanding of the long-term implications of current actions.

The Causes of Declining CSW

I hope at this point, you are beginning to understand the overwhelming importance of a high, and constantly increasing, level of Collective Societal Wisdom among groups as small as corporate teams, to entire societies in every corner of the globe. Of course, increasing CSW is never an easy thing as every society has different sizes, cultures, resources, geography, governments, etc. There are an unlimited number of factors that can contribute to each and every community of people that go into increasing CSW. The question becomes how to ensure that the CSW of a population is growing in a healthy way.

One way to start is to avidly avoid allowing CSW to decline. So, then what causes CSW to decrease?

There are only two factors guaranteed to cause a decline in CSW: the loss of authentic interconnectivity among people within the population, and the loss of creativity among the general population. I will explain both of these factors and why they are important much more in depth later in the book but for now let me at least define the terms.

When I say interconnectivity, I do not mean the number of followers you have on social media, or the number of people you have met in person. Authentic interconnectivity is the capacity and fluidity of the flow of knowledge, perspectives, cultures, and freedom of those within a society as well as with those in a different society, and even the interconnectivity between multiple societies on a global scale.

The same response underlies the loss of both interconnectivity and creativity: Fear. Fear is the root cause of almost every societal problem of any community or nation anywhere in the world. Fear is generally the emotional response to the uncertainty or the unknown. Many people feel uncertain or afraid of the future because they do not know what the future will bring, which of course nobody knows. Therefore, many individuals, who fear for themselves in the future, attempt to be like what those in power want them to be.

One source of power in modern capitalist societies are the corporations, which promise long and fruitful careers to those who study exactly what the corporation wants them to study, build exactly what skills the corporation wants them to build, and participate in activities that the corporation tells them to participate in. In doing this, the corporation creates the perfect worker for exactly the tiny niche job that the corporation thinks it may need, while the individual eliminates some of his fear of the unknown future because he believes in the corporation's promise of success. In addition, the fact that the corporation, or some other person or entity, tells this individual exactly what he needs to do to have a successful future, further diminishes his fear of the unknown because now he is not wondering what he needs to do to have a great future, he is simply being told.

This may sound great for that individual but there are a few major implications that this style of building the next generation of worker has for society, which relate directly to the two factors that decrease CSW, the loss of interconnectivity and the loss of creativity.

When it comes to learning, which of course is a significant factor of CSW whether it's learning factual knowledge, perspectives, cultural practices, political systems, or any other type of learning, the vast majority of learning comes from another person. Either in the form of verbally teaching or in the form of a book or video, which of course was created by someone, a lot of learning comes from people.

The other way of learning is learning by experience, which I will talk about in the next chapter when we discuss how we know about all these factors I have been describing and how they interact together. But for this chapter, most learning comes from other people. And the knowledge and perspectives and attitudes of these people who are teaching you, have also been passed on through other people. They surely have added their own ideas and perspectives to this information but ultimately everything is passed along from other human beings.

Hence, it becomes quite clear that to get an intellectual edge, you simply must learn from as many people as possible. In other words, you must meet and talk to and get to know the stories of as many people as possible. This is interconnectivity. Genuine, face-to-face interaction without a specific agenda other than building a relationship.

Furthermore, a huge percentage of learning does not come from active learning. If you are talking to someone without specifically thinking, "I am trying to learn certain things," you will learn much that you would not otherwise have learned from attending a class. This is because teachers in classrooms have a set curriculum and often do not provide other perspectives. In other words, they must always be on guard to keep the class within certain curricular limits. Traditional schooling is of course important to learn basic skills such as mathematics and grammar. However, if you are talking to an individual outside of an academic setting, there are numerous important things that you can learn, and on a more personal and relatable level.

Personal connections like these all make up the interconnectivity of a society. As I stated earlier, interconnectivity is the fluidity and rate of the flow of knowledge. If you increase everybody's number of connections by even one, the fluidity of knowledge increases exponentially because each person now has new information which can then be passed on to other new or old connections, who then pass on this new knowledge while adding their own ideas, thus creating new knowledge on a greater scale of network.

Running directly alongside societal interconnectivity is the notion of creativity, which can also be defined as the capacity to innovate. It is already well-known that traditional institutions such as corporate settings or public classrooms generally stifle creativity but not many people can explain why. Many people find it difficult to pinpoint the cause of declining creativity for two reasons: the first is that creativity is an invisible force and therefore quite difficult to measure quantitatively. Things that are difficult to measure quantitatively thus become difficult to finance. The second is that people are simply thinking too hard about it. Let me flesh it out for you.

Everybody knows that each individual is born with a natural curiosity and extremely active creative drive. Studies have claimed to have found the part of the brain used for creative purposes. We all have seen the wildly free imaginations of children in the form of art, imaginary games, or even just the things they say. Children have not yet been molded by the confines of societal norms which allows them to create and innovate at an output unmatched by almost any adult mind. Most of us take this for granted.

It is also common to talk about the midlife crisis of the adult who has been working at the same company for thirty years who may have had promotions, but his job was essentially the same job with a bigger cubicle. The age old question has always been this: at what point does the creativity and imagination that all children own so gallantly get suppressed, thus transforming that carefree child into an almost machine-like worker of adulthood whose life consists of receiving tasks and completing them and receiving more tasks and completing them endlessly.

The first reason that creativity gets almost completely diminished by the time people reach adulthood is because there is this longstanding idea that creativity is not profitable and is thus not worth encouraging, let alone augmenting. Because of this false notion, the public-school system has eliminated creative enhancement from their curriculums and, as stated above, corporations have been continuously increasing specialization to the level where each worker has exactly one job and one reason for being at the company and if this worker goes outside his tiny sphere, he is punished.

Before I get into explaining how ridiculous the notion is that creativity is not profitable, I would like to also highlight the hypocrisy of the American sphere, where I reside, particularly in the business world. I'm sure you all know someone who has grown up with their parents saying, "Well son, your music playing is great and your art is great and I know you love it very much, but let's be realistic, you're not ever going to make any money from those creative things. You need to learn finance"

Now this may or may not be true that Billy is not going to make any money directly from his artwork. However, what he is doing is maintaining and stimulating that creative part of his brain. This can be unbelievably profitable. In fact, the companies who went out of their way to stimulate creativity, which they called innovation, became so profitable that every business in every corner of the world began to use the term. In 2015, innovation was the number one most-used business buzzword in the world according to Meltwater's online analysis (Keating, 2015). For those of you who believe that innovation is different than creativity, I have provided the definition of "innovate" given by

Merriam-Webster Dictionary as well as the definition of "create" for comparison.

Innovation: "the introduction of something new"

Create: "to bring into existence"

"To bring into existence" suggests that it is new because it did not exist before. And innovation is the act of introducing something new. These definitions make it is abundantly clear that innovation and creation are identical actions. But why so many businesses and schools want people to be able to innovate but at the same time are deliberately stifling the creative arts, otherwise known as the liberal arts, is truly baffling

Anyway, let's get back to explaining how creativity can be profitable both for the individual and for the community. Again, note that "community" can mean a work group, an entire business, or a whole nation. This idea is not something difficult to comprehend but for some reason many people overthink this, or at least do not connect the dots. Back to innovation in the business world. Everybody knows that innovation is extraordinarily important in the business world, and is arguably one, if not the most profitable factor of a business. Think about the most successful businesses today. They have all been either the first to do something or they took something and changed it into something new and better.

For example:

Apple: the first to give us the idea of a visual computer "desktop" and the first to combine a cellphone with music and other things, thus creating the smartphone.

Google: the first to make a truly simple way to surf the internet and find what you are looking for with the least amount of effort possible.

Facebook: not the first social media company, but the first to provide fun things such as the like button and relationship status.

Coca-Cola: the first company to bottle soda.

You get the point.

Each of these companies created something new, either from scratch, or more likely from something already out there, that they learned about through their connections. Furthermore, they have been able to continue to adapt to the changing world by further innovating to stay relevant and keep up the edge. Nobody likes a company that comes out with nothing new. Imagine if Ford was still selling the Model T today exactly as it was in 1908 and had been doing so every year since then. Would anyone be commuting to work or driving their kids to school in that car?

Creativity is profitable. Companies able to continuously create and adapt stay profitable. And furthermore, creativity can be exceptionally profitable for the individual as well. Obviously, all these wonderfully innovative companies, who either produce creative products such as Apple or function in a way that was never seen before such as Uber, are centered around people. People are the ones coming up with these great ideas. If you work for a company, at absolutely any level, there is nothing more profitable for you personally than helping the company make more profits. If you are able to come up with even the tiniest, simplest idea to increase output, even only for you individually, higher-ups will notice and reward you over the long term.

Again, even if you are only creative enough to find ways to increase your own output, you will be greatly rewarded. The vast majority of workers simply do as they are told and complete tasks exactly as they are told in exactly the amount of time they are told. But if an individual can change one little aspect that makes him or her increase his own productivity by even 1%, he is suddenly at least 1% more profitable than almost everyone else at that company. This makes that worker indispensable. If economic times come crashing down and layoffs are issued, the head honchos will certainly not let that person go.

Say the average worker earns the company about $100,000 per year but you, using your creative mind, have come up with a clever time management system to make you get about 1% more work done each day. This means you are making the company $110,000 per year. Despite what you may think, the bosses notice this. Not only does it make you look good, but a boss of an extremely productive person looks very good as well. Therefore, in no way will your boss give you up as a worker when almost every other worker only makes $100,000 for the company. Thinking outside the box, even on a tiny scale, can have huge rewards and thus it is vital to constantly be using and exercising the creative part of your brain.

Creativity must be allowed to flow through all aspects of society. However, let me further stress how dangerous declining creativity can be for a society. As I explained, innovation/creativity is one of the most important factors in increasing societal outputs socially and economically. Hence declining innovation directly leads to a decrease in output which leads to, at best, stagnation. Stagnation, in any aspect of society, can be a lethal blow for long-term welfare.

Let's discuss stagnation in the economic sense, which is generally what most of the Western capitalists want to talk about. Umair Haque, in his article "Why the World is Ripping Itself Apart," describes a chilling finding and its effect on societies throughout history, including those of today. The finding, from 2018, is this: One-third of Americans would give up their right to vote for a 10% raise which, looking at average American incomes, translates to about $5000 (Brown, 2018). As Haque explains, if a leader comes along and offers this exact trade, many Americans will quite easily take the offer, thus eliminating democracy in a single move.

Haque writes that essentially this means economic stagnation leads people to turn to authoritarian figures. These figures promise the general population increased economic output in exchange for freedoms. Looking at the aftermath of the Great Depression in the 1930's, this theory was proven even in well-educated nations such as Germany, Japan, and Russia (Haque, 2018). And unfortunately, as many around the world are still trying to recover from the Great Recession, we see the same thing happening today, even in well-educated nations such as Russia, the UK, and the United States.

Overall, stagnation, which arises from the lack of innovation, leads to growing fear. Fear then leads to narrow-mindedness and isolation. As we get more and more afraid, we cut off connections, and become more and more isolated. As we get more isolated, we have less interchange of knowledge, perspectives, and ideas, which forces us to make assumptions about those with whom we have cutoff contact. Assumptions quickly transform into blatant misinformation, which in turn leads to more fear because, as we know, fear stems from groups, information, perspectives, or ideas, that are either unknown or misunderstood. Thus, fear can swiftly snowball into more and more fear, which will only grow exponentially if unmanaged and severely diminish the CSW of a society.

Of course, many people wonder what the solution is for growing fear. It is simpler than most people think. Fear stems from the unknown, the misunderstood, and misinformation. Therefore, the logical solution to all of those is education. Education makes things known, helps people understand, and provides better information. Quality education is the single most effective, and long-lasting, solution for fear, which I will explain in much more detail later in the book.

History: Looking at the Answer Sheet During the Test

The previous chapters all describe the relationship between fear, interconnectivity or isolation, and CSW, but the question becomes this: How do we know all this to be true? And furthermore, knowing that this relationship is true, how can societies act in a way that they can maintain a healthy path of existence, or at least improve the path they are currently traversing?

The answer is simple. We must look at history. How does a child learn that fire is hot? Yes, generally their parents will of course warn them not to touch the fry pan over the flame, but the child will never truly know how hot fire can be until he inevitably touches the pan. From that point on, that child will do everything in his power not to touch objects over a flame ever again. That experience will create such a powerful memory in his mind that it will surpass the strength of anything his parents may have taught him. In other words, humans learn best by experience. This is an evolutionary tactic that all high-intelligence animals have: the ability to learn from experience and avoid past mistakes.

In fact, one such issue in most of the developed world is that modern societies have become hugely performance-based. Thus, children are taught from an early age that mistakes are wrong and can even be punished for making mistakes. However, if mistakes are the most effective learning tool for humans, scaring children out of making mistakes is actually eliminating their most powerful learning tool. Additionally, punishing mistakes eliminates creativity. Again, if children are afraid to make a mistake, they will certainly not do anything outside of what is considered the "right thing to do."

In much of the developed world, adult workers are discouraged from trying new ways to work by the fear of punishment for low performance, yet ironically businesses have been promoting the idea of innovation. How can one create something new if he or she is punished for trying something new and failing? As we all know, most innovations or inventions are mistakes themselves.

Societies are created by humans, and thus act like humans. Therefore, just as individuals learn from their past mistakes and successes, societies must do the same as well. Communities of all sizes can do this by looking at history. History is the wisdom of everyone and every community before us and reveals the consequences of their decisions and actions for themselves, those around them, and those who came after them.

Essentially, as societies travel through time, coming across issues along the way, chances are there are parallel issues that have been faced by societies in the past. By looking at history, modern people and societies as a whole can see what worked or what failed in the past when a previous society came across a similar issue. Simply put, societies have the answers to the majority of problems that they face if they would only look at the past.

Most of this book focuses on the American Empire, its residents, and its actions. Luckily for the Americans, there was once a great empire that maintained the most sophisticated and widespread military in the world, its currency was the universal currency, its people were proud, and its power and influence spread across the entirety of the known world at the time. That society was known as the Roman Empire. The American and Roman Empires share many of the same values and because of this, act in similar ways as well[5] (See Further Readings). Almost every major issue the United States has faced, or will face in the future, there is a high chance the Roman Empire faced the same.

Unfortunately, the Romans did not have a past society as similar to them as the Americans are to them. Hence, the Romans made many mistakes as they traversed through the societal life-cycle, before they ultimately collapsed and brought the western world into the Dark Ages. Sadly, the United States has been making many of the same mistakes the Romans did in the decades before the Empire collapsed.

Before describing these issues in Part II, I will quickly describe some of the major similarities between the Roman and American Empires. Many modern folks feel they are much more sophisticated, or at the very least different, than the generations that lived thousands of years ago, however, this is not the case. Citizens of the Roman Empire had many identical values, sense of humor, interests, and feelings that modern Americans have today.

On a societal level, one of the most significant similarities between the United States and the Roman Empire is that both nations are massive warmongers. The Roman Empire was at war for a massive percentage of their existence as the Roman Republic or Empire.

Notable Roman wars include: the Roman-Etruscan wars (where the Romans decided the Etruscan land was actually the Roman homeland much like the Americans did with the Native Americans), the Samnite Wars the Pyrrhic War, the three Punic Wars, the four Macedonian Wars, the Social War, the Gallic Wars, the Parthian Wars, the Dacian Wars, the Persian Wars, the Gothic Wars, the war with the Huns, among many others.

Many Americans know that the Romans valued wars and conquest quite highly but fail to realize that the United States is almost identical. In 2019, the United States has been around for 243 years. Within those 243 years, the United States has actually only been at peace for 21 years. In other words, the United States has been at war for 93% of its entire existence.

Notable American wars include: the Revolutionary War, the Chickamuaga Wars, the Quasi-War, the Barbary Wars, the Seminole Wars, the Cherokee Wars, the Mexican-American War, the Texas-Indian Wars, the American Civil War, the Apache Wars, the Philippine-American War, the Banana Wars, WWI, WWII, the Korean War, the Vietnam War, the CIA proxy wars in Afghanistan, the Gulf War, the Iraq war, the War on Terror in Afghanistan, and many more.

Because of so many conquests throughout their histories, both Roman and American societies became almost entirely made up of foreigners. In the United States, only 1.3% of the entire population is actually Native to American soil (United States Census Bureau, 2018). Furthermore, both societies claim to be "democratic republics" with the

American government system being heavily influenced, and in some areas directly copied, from the Roman government of the Republic (before the imperial stage).

Even the American voting systems such as geographical gerrymandering or the electoral college come from the voting assemblies of the Roman Republic. In Rome, there were three separate voting assemblies, the Comitia Centuriata, Comitia Tribuna, and the Concilia Plebis.

The Comitia Centuriata would assemble to elect officials such as the consul. The Roman populace was divided into 193 groups, with each group representing one vote, for a total of 193 votes. To determine which vote each group, or century, would place, votes within each group took place. This is quite similar to the functioning of the electoral college. Of course, citizens were divided up based on net worth, thus giving the wealthy Romans control of the majority of the centuries, despite the process seeming somewhat democratic. Furthermore, Roman elections began with the richest centuries voting first, and as soon as there was a majority decision, the remaining groups were not allowed to vote.

The Comitia Tribuna assembly was made up of 35 geographic districts based on where civilians resided. There were four urban districts and 31 rural districts. This committee elected certain officials and voted on much legislation. The vote functioning was similar to the previous voting system, although all votes must be placed in the city of Rome, without any sort of absentee ballot. Traveling to the city took significant amounts of time and money, which most Romans could not afford, therefore giving the wealthy a massive advantage in votes. Furthermore, the less wealthy Romans who actually lived in the city of Rome could vote easily but they could only possibly control the 4 urban districts compared to the 31 others.

The Romans did have an electoral body known as the Concilia Plebis, in which the wealthy people of status were not allowed to participate. However, the only power this body had was to elect tribunes, who functioned as judges to check the power of the senators and other government officials (Aldrete, 2008).

The manipulation of the voting system by the upper-class Romans reveals striking similarities to that of the American system. Gerrymandering, or artificially drawing district lines to exclude voting power for certain groups, is a well-known example of vote manipulation in the United States. Furthermore, just as the Romans made it difficult for most people to actually be present during voting times, the US uses the same techniques.

For example, holding elections on Tuesdays, when the working class has to work, makes it deliberately difficult for the working class to vote. The conservative strategy of closing down voting booths in minority neighborhoods to make travelling to vote more of a hassle and lines at voting booths longer is another strategy quite similar to the Romans. Forcing people to travel, takes time out of their days, or to skip work to vote will certainly limit votes.

However, not all Roman and American comparisons are negative. Just as the United States provides social welfare services such as the Supplemental Nutrition Assistance Program, or SNAP, the Roman Empire provided significant welfare services for its people, the most famous being the grain dole. From the first century BC throughout the imperial era, the Roman administration presented every male citizen with 5 modii of grain every month, or the equivalent of around 3500 calories per day (Parkin & Pomeroy, 2007).

Not only are the government systems designed the same but the regular civilians of the Roman Empire shared many of the same interests as Americans do. For example, the Romans were sports fanatics. The most popular sports in the Roman era were arena sports and chariot racing much like the US loves arena sports such as American football and racing events with lots of crashes like NASCAR.

The Romans also enjoyed theatre, music performances, and even political satire. In fact, it turns out the Romans shared many of the same humorous thoughts as modern folk do. For instance, Mary Beard in her 2012 documentary, "Meet the Romans," reveals graffiti scrawled across the walls of a public Roman restroom. Some of this graffiti depicts famous historical figures engaging in "potty-mouth" conversation (Beard, 2012).

Despite the common misconception that people thousands of years ago were tremendously different and suffered different problems in their day-to-day lives, people back then still had the same brains, same values, same thoughts and feelings, and the same struggles as many of us today. The civilians living during the time of the Roman Empire were quite similar, and at times just as arrogant about their sophistication, as Americans today.

Because of this, societies, their leaders, and their citizens must remember that solutions to modern issues can be discovered by looking in the past. Furthermore, mistakes made in the past must also be studied in order for our current societies to avoid making the same mistakes again. This framework will be used to discuss a variety of issues in the modern era, particularly in the United States, in the remainder of this book.

PART II

The Importance of Interconnectivity and How Isolationism Leads to Declining Collective Societal Wisdom

The Importance of Interconnectivity

You now understand the nature of Collective Societal Wisdom, how CSW impacts societal progress, how interconnectivity impacts CSW, and finally how we know all these factors and their connections to be accurate. Now it is time to get into the details.

I briefly described the significance of interconnectivity and dangers of isolation in a previous chapter, but we are now ready to delve in deeper as well as analyze actual real-world situations showing how interconnectivity and its opposite counterpart, isolation, can impact societies in a massive way.

Imagine a single, isolated brain-cell, or neuron. Imagine that this neuron is the biggest, best, most efficient neuron the world has ever seen. This neuron has the ability to complete all of its tasks with perfect execution with maximum output and minimum effort and can do this in record time. There is no other existing neuron that could outperform this neuron in any way at doing whatever it does.

However, this neuron is isolated. Even though this neuron is powerful and efficient, without connections allowing for the trade and transfer of information with other neurons from other parts of the brain that are doing different things and hold different information, this neuron is rendered utterly useless in helping the rest of the brain.

Without connections, the neuron cannot transfer the products resulting from its genius to the rest of the brain to be used for large-scale actions requiring numerous neurons. This makes the rest of the brain much less efficient if it is not running at full capacity. Additionally, without communication channels the neuron cannot receive information or input from other neurons that may have different information. Thus, how does the neuron know what actions should come next if it does not fully understand the outside situation or what the brain as a whole is trying to accomplish. And most importantly, without strong connections, the neuron cannot show other neurons how to do certain things as efficiently as it does. In other words, our neuron cannot teach the other neurons to improve and thus the other neurons cannot learn the skills of our awesome neuron.

The transfer of information between individuals, otherwise known as teaching, is extraordinarily important for the progress of society. Regarding our neurons, if every neuron in the brain could learn even a few things from the best neuron, the entire brain would increase its power and efficiency many times over. Furthermore, since each neuron holds different information and has different skillsets, the constant interchanging of information between all neurons would so dramatically increase the power of the entire system that it would be almost impossible to measure.

In comparison, a brain that has a limited number of connections, or poor quality of connections, would be running at a level that would be only a tiny fraction of the brain's full potential capacity. It quickly becomes obvious that the connections between the neurons are much more important than the power of the individual neurons themselves. There are so many neurons in the brain that of course some will be extremely productive, and some will be lazy and ineffective. However, the connections increase the entire brain power without trying to find and improve the bad neurons individually.

All this has been well-known to those within the medical field for some time. Many children even learn about neurons in their science classes, which teach the significance of the axon, through which signals are sent, and how each neuron has numerous dendrites, which are receiving ports for signals from other neurons, suggesting that neurons are designed to receive many, many signals by making countless connections. This is all common knowledge in the medical field.

However, for whatever reason, this idea of connections being more important than individual capacity seems to be lacking in many other fields of study, particularly in analysis of large-scale systems such as entire societies. There actually is no larger, more complex system on Earth than the human brain and therefore I strongly defend the idea that the brain should be the analogous starting point for any systemic analysis in any field.

The human brain is made up of more than 100 billion individual neurons, many times more individuals than the entire population of the world, each with numerous connections, with some estimates putting the total number of synaptic connections in one brain at 1000 trillion connections. That's right, 1000 trillion. Therefore, the idea that societies are too complex to analyze empirically and instead must be analyzed using theories is false. The human brain is a conveniently sized, exceptionally complex system that we can analyze empirically as much as we want. This research could then be applied to look at the workings of entire societies.

Furthermore, the brain has other aspects that make it a useful analogy to compare with entire societies. We all know that societies, and the entire world for that matter, have so many different pieces and aspects that they influence and so many factors that influence them. Some of these pieces of society include the culture, the resources, the population, the government, the economy, the diplomatic relations, the military, the education, the political borders etc. This is just like the brain. Except the brain has many more. The brain has different parts that do different things as well including motor skills (economic output), personality (culture), memory (education), social skills (diplomatic relations), providing survival skills such as the drive to eat and stay hydrated (acquiring resources), making sure the heart and lungs are always supplying the brain with oxygen, so it can continue to function (collecting taxes) etc.

Before I get carried away, let me reiterate. The brain is the most complex system in the world and there is thus no better system than the brain to use in analyzing how systems function and what causes them to progress. The single most important aspect of the brain, and the reason that the brain is so powerful, is its connections. Furthermore, among separate brains, the more powerful brains are proven to have stronger, and higher quality connections than the lesser brains. Thus, increasing interconnectivity directly increases brainpower while increasing the level of isolation among individual neurons or clusters of neurons decreases brainpower. The book, *Micro-, Meso- and Macro-Connectomics of the Brain*, describes in extreme detail the effects of healthy connections within the brain, even regarding seemingly non-physical aspects of life such as social interaction[6] (See Further Readings).

Using this knowledge, we can see how societies function identically. Increase interconnectivity and the society will improve every aspect it holds relation to. Consequently, increasing isolationist policies and over-encouraging individualism will swiftly decrease societal output and its long-term well-being.

For the vast majority of civilization, humans have lived in villages, or small towns, with multiple generations all residing in the same place. This allowed for the easy transfer of knowledge and experience from the older generations to the younger, which continued consistently without issue. However, the younger generations of the world today increasingly want to be more and more independent at a younger and younger age. Strong ambition and healthy independence can be extremely powerful if used properly, but many members of the younger generations in particular have a flawed definition of the term independence.

More and more people consider full independence to mean being fully self-sustaining and requiring no support from anyone at any point. This can all look great in theory but if you live in a community larger than the Dunbar number[7] (See Further Readings), no one can be truly self-sustaining. Furthermore, it is just about impossible for any individual to find success completely alone. Successful people have always built strong relationships, actively searched out mentors to help them even after their success, and constantly maintain a strong network of support.

The saying goes, "One can only stand tall by standing on the shoulders of giants." This same ideology applies to entire societies. There is not a single nation in the world that functions as completely self-sufficient. In fact, the wealthiest countries in the world by GDP have the highest volume of trade with other nations.

For example, the five richest nations in the world by nominal GDP are ranked in the following order: United States, China, Japan, Germany, United Kingdom. Each of these nations receive between 13% and 42% of their GDP from trading, which amounts to trillions of dollars (WTO Statistics Database, n.d.). Therefore, movements within the UK, Germany, and the United States that have developed seeking trade limits, increased tariffs and other policies to directly decrease trade, or at least incentivize a trade decrease represents a serious contradiction to their cause. In 2017, the United States GDP per capita was just over $57,000 and over $7,700 of that came from trade (United States of

America Trade Profile, n.d.). Most Americans would not want to erase $7,700 in economic output for every single person in the United States.

The decrease in economic output also does not include the increased cost of consumer goods that policies such as tariffs would create. Recently in the United States there was a proposal to create a 25% tariff on imported steel and 10% on aluminum. In 2017, the US imported steel from 85 different countries amounting to over 30 million metric tons of steel. Steel is used in countless products made in the US, and the demand for steel continues to grow. The International Trade Administration's Steel Imports Report of the United States claims, "Since 2009, apparent consumption (a measure of steel demand) has consistently exceeded production." Between 2010 and 2018, crude steel production (not including US exports) in the United States grew from 80.5 mmt (million metric tons) to 86.6 mmt – a 7.6% increase, while apparent consumption increased over 20% during the same time, going from 90.7 mmt to 109.0 mmt (Steel Imports Report: United States, 2019).

Given this information, it becomes quite clear that domestic US steel production cannot keep up with even a fraction of the total US demand for steel, so of course the US must import. But if tariffs are raised on all steel imports, the prices for the millions of products built with steel will go up as well. For example, we could see a 25% price increase of an

American-made car. Of course, in reality, the percentage increase to the consumer would not necessarily equate to the increase to wholesale price, but the price increases will surely reach the consumer eventually.

Societies and their levels of interconnectivity do not only refer to physical goods, however. Just like the human brain, information is the most important commodity that must be traded and transferred. One example that has not been covered by the media nearly as much as it should be is the relationship between pharmaceutical companies and healthcare professionals.

The last few decades have brought about a legal drug explosion around the world, but particularly in the US where regulation for new medication is much less strict that in other developed nations. There is a medication for everything and everyone of all ages. The medication invasion has been so massive over the last twenty years that two of the top five best performing stocks over the last twenty years have been pharmaceutical companies. One of these companies, Celgene, outperformed the annual stock gains of both Apple and Google over the twenty-year period from 1996-2016. From February 1996, Celgene share prices rose from a mere 70 cents to around $100 in 2016 accounting for a whopping 28% compounding annual return. Gilead Sciences, the other pharmaceutical company represented on the top five list, provided 24%

compounding annual returns from Feb. 1996 to 2016 (Downie, 2016). For comparison, Amazon was not even on this list in 2016.

In other words, a gigantic explosion of pharmaceutical activity has overtaken the world of caretaking with little input from actual medical professionals[8] (See Further Readings).

Given the significance of the drug bubble in the United States, let me explain how this may be impacting the American population. There are clearly millions of people being medicated in the US to keep these companies' revenues growing so rapidly and consistently. But are there really that many health problems requiring medication in the United States? And furthermore, does anyone really know the long-term health costs of all this medication?

There is one way to find out. The logical way would be for the pharmaceutical companies to ask the healthcare professionals how their drugs actually work on patients because the doctors are generally in charge of long-term care for patients rather than the simple tests the drug companies run. In fact, tests on the long-term health effects should be funded and implemented to ensure that the drugs aren't causing more problems in the future that would require more drugs. Or maybe people needing more drugs is not a bad thing for these drug companies.

Of course, there are many amazing drugs out there for all sorts of previously incurable diseases such as cancer or HIV. If a patient contracts a potentially fatal disease, the drugs' long-term health effects do not matter anymore. But what about, for example, the tens of thousands of preteen boys who are being diagnosed with ADHD because they cannot sit still in class (as if that is a problem requiring drug use) and are thus heavily medicated with amphetamines as if that solves all their "problems."

These children are deliberately turned into amphetamine addicts from a tremendously young age, and an age where they have not fully matured, which means of course they have a tough time sitting still and doing their schoolwork. Furthermore, these boys are told that their inability to sit through school is a "problem." Almost all young boys are bundles of energy and thus should be allowed to have longer recesses and play sports after school and other physically active ways to burn off energy rather than just jumping to medication. In fact, the vast majority of health professionals have agreed that exercise is the single greatest tool for both physical and mental health.

With regards to children, studies have shown that increased exercise increases focus and attention span, and even actual student grades in school[9] (See Further Readings). Therefore, rather than quickly blaming and medicating young boys for having too much energy, policies could be implemented to make the education system friendlier towards those with a lot of energy.

This is also important because many successful and charismatic adults are known for having high energy and those who are lethargic or have low energy output are usually much less successful both socially and financially. Hence, why should the system be designed to suppress energy and enthusiasm from an early age instead of learning to channel that energy into one's productivity and social skills?

Some may argue that medicating these boys provides focus. However, are the boys playing around during class really un-focused? Or are they simply focusing on what they see as more fun and more rewarding? They are "thinking outside the box," which is a powerful skill and should be allowed to flourish. Of course, these boys should be taught boundaries so they are not hurting or bothering other students, but there should be other ways besides medicating them to help them learn social skills and other life skills.

As stated earlier, the scariest part of the medication invasion is that there has been such limited research on the long-term effects of these drugs. For these boys who are medicated for ADHD, no one really knows the long-term implications of taking high doses of amphetamines every day from the age of 6 or 7. However, if the pharmaceutical companies and the healthcare professionals got together and exchanged this information, everybody would be healthier. The pharmaceutical companies would have to turn to doing more research on drugs to cure more dangerous diseases, in other words innovate, in order to make up for profit-loss from decreasing ADHD medication production which would be better for everybody. Subsequently, children would be happier and healthier without being drugged every day. Furthermore, if the healthcare professionals had more information exchange with school administration, more physical activity could be added to school systems to further increase student grades and graduation rates.

The issue with this is that in some people's minds, the drugs "work" in the short term. Children are being sedated to sit still in their seats, however the deeper costs of this approach are not usually apparent to the parties involved.

The ADHD example revealing the lack of interconnectivity between two massive fields, the medical field and the biopharmaceutical industry, which run directly alongside each other, is only one small example. There are countless examples in the real world that show how increased interconnectivity can bring about benefits for everyone. In fact, just about every aspect of society can benefit from striving to increase the fluidity of information among individuals and entire communities.

The importance of interconnectivity becomes even further highlighted by looking at the most innovative solutions to global or societal problems. We circle back to innovation and creativity. The fact of the matter is that creativity is simply the action of mixing and matching old knowledge with other old knowledge to create new knowledge. The most creative solutions combine knowledge from different areas of study, or different industries, or different cultures.

We briefly discussed the profitability of creativity earlier in the book, but let's take a look at how the mixing of knowledge created amazing innovations such as radiation therapy for cancer treatment. This is one of the most widely used and most effective treatments for cancer, which of course is global health issue.

Radiation therapy consists of using a linear particle accelerator to create high-energy beams of subatomic particles which damage the DNA within the cells of a tumor, leading to the deaths of the cancerous cells. By using multiple angles of these beams, with the ends of the beams culminating into one specific spot, this radiation can be hyper-focused on the actual tumor with less damage done to the surrounding tissue. This is undoubtedly a brilliant invention. But it was not created by medical professionals alone.

The journey to radiation therapy starts in the mid-1800s with the invention of the incandescent lightbulb, patented by none other than Thomas Edison, although over twenty other inventors had built working incandescent lightbulbs before him. The success of the vacuum-sealed lightbulb sparked further experiments with electricity within an airtight container, eventually leading to the invention of the true vacuum tube in the first few years of the 20th century. The vacuum tube is simply an airtight vessel containing at least two electrodes, allowing for some type of electrical activity.

Vacuum tubes sparked further interest from physicists, eventually resulting in the Crookes tube, invented by William Crookes by 1875. The Crookes tube was a partial vacuum tube that allowed one to see cathode rays, which are streams of electrons travelling uninterrupted by any other gas atom floating within the tube. Because there were no other atoms to stop the electrons, they accelerated to incredibly high speeds, and would eventually crash into the end of the tube, resulting in a glow. However, at the time, these rays were not known to be electrons.

Eventually, experiments with more cathode ray tubes resulted in the discovery of the electron by J.J. Thomson in 1897. Moving forward to the 1920s, the concept of the linear particle accelerator was invented by Gustav Ising, whose early academic background was in philosophy, receiving his B.A. in the subject from Uppsala University. His idea was brought into reality a few years later by Rolf Widerøe.

Around the same time, X-rays were beginning to be used as cancer treatments by Emil Grubbe in Chicago. However, in the 1940s, linear particle accelerators were taken from the physics world and built for medical purposes, thus bringing radiation therapy into the modern era.

All of the exchanges of information from seemingly irrelevant fields of study resulted in the invention of a hugely successful medical treatment that could theoretically be used for anybody around the world. The openness to try new things and combine information from multiple fields of study created something new. Imagine if the medical world did not think it was relevant to look at tools for physics experiments such as the linear particle accelerator.

Interconnectivity between individuals, systems, and societies is essential for the exchange of ideas and information, which produce new ideas and information, ultimately leading to societal progress.

The Dangers of Isolationism

As described above, increasing interconnectivity can vastly improve long-term output and benefits for all levels of society. Despite this fact, increasing interconnectivity is not always possible. Unfortunately, many people in the Western hemisphere believe that decreasing interconnectivity is better for everyone. Ideas that are designed to decrease interconnectivity can be defined as Isolationist Ideas. This chapter explains the serious dangers of isolationist movements and mindsets to single societies as well as the world.

Using the brain example from the previous chapter, we remember that the connections of the brain are of the utmost importance and in fact directly relate to overall brainpower and capacity. Furthermore, an individual neuron requires connections to be able to know and understand what is going on in the rest of the system for the cell and system to function properly.

Without far-reaching connections, or any connections at all, the neuron only knows the situation in its own tiny little world. The entire body could be fighting pancreatic cancer, but this neuron could have absolutely no idea that the system it belongs to is literally fighting for its life. Because of this, that neuron does not know what the best action would be to help the rest of the body because, from where this neuron is, everything seems perfectly normal, at least for now.

Now imagine that whole groups of neurons decided they wanted to "be independent" and isolate themselves from the rest of the brain and thus the rest of the body. If this happens, there would not be enough brain cells to direct the body at full function which may cause the cancer to take over. Because of this selfishness, the entire body, including those "independent" neurons (which of course are not really independent because they still require water and oxygen and other services from the rest of the system) will die much quicker than they would have if they had worked together to try and solve the problem.

Again, this idea can be applied to society. Ultimately, isolation leads to misinformation and thus misunderstanding. When an individual, or a whole community, cuts off connections from the rest of the system (read: world), they become extremely misinformed because there is no transfer of knowledge or information from the outside. Maybe everything looks completely fine in this particular community and things are going well for them, but they could be completely oblivious to outside forces or events that could have drastic impacts on their entire community. If this does happen, that particular community would be swept up in whatever the issue is by total surprise without any preparation.

The same result can happen when connections are simply ignored as well. This exact result happened during the year leading up to the 2016 presidential election in the United States. As the now-current president was gaining momentum, the majority of democrats ignored all the signs of trouble because they believed, "Well I know better, this will never happen." And thus numerous people were so unprepared for the actual election because too many people refused to acknowledge information from outside their own community.

Misinformation, whether it is from the lack of connections, inaccurate or invalid connections, or simply ignoring accurate connections, can be absolutely devastating to the well-being of a society. This is because decisions are all made based on some sort of information. However, decisions that are made based on inaccurate, or limited information can cause devastating consequences, even if these consequences do not appear for some time.

Currently, many in the United States, as well as other developed nations, know that unbelievable numbers of people are hugely misinformed about almost every important subject. The massive media coverage of, and participation in, the "fake news" spectacle began to highlight how widespread misinformation really is around the world, even in so-called educated nations.

So, the question becomes this: *How can so many people be misinformed in the Age of Information?*

Arguably the single most significant phenomenon impacting a population's collective misinformation is something that I have termed the Tragedy of Isolated Perspective, or TIP. The Tragedy of Isolated Perspective defines the series of events and miscommunications due to a lack of strong connections between communities. This results in misunderstandings between the communities and their reasons for their actions. Due to the lack of accurate information and understanding, both communities come to their own assumed conclusions, which again do not take into account the information of the other community due to the lack of connections and thus information, and are therefore usually inaccurate, as to what the values of the other community are and why the other community is doing what they were doing.

Thus, both communities essentially make up their own information about the other community without considering the perspectives of that community. This leads to a further decrease in inter-community connections as the misinformation spreads and evolves, as all information does, among each community but stays isolated in each separate community. Eventually, each community is only acting on its own information, whether or not that information is accurate, without taking into account any other information or perspective from the other community, thus only acting upon its own isolated perspective.

TIP applies to both communities and individuals, as most phenomena do. Let's take a look at some real-world examples of both. First, consider TIP among individuals and what it looked like historically in the form of the extraordinarily popular idea of cult religion in ancient Roman times since, as many people forget, societies hundreds or thousands of years ago had the exact same issues as societies today. TIP is no different. We can compare the historical example of misinformation due to isolation to the modern marvel known as social media. Ironically, both of these quickly caused entire populations to become misinformed, which can be illustrated with some real-world examples of TIP in entire communities.

In the first couple centuries of the common era, the Roman Empire was the largest, wealthiest, and most advanced civilization in the world. As in any wealthy and powerful nation of global proportion, there was a wage gap of unimaginable scope, and most people were so caught up in making a living that they had little time for other pleasurable activities. In many cases, the stress and pressure of living in a rich, advanced society crushes the will of many people because they were constantly comparing themselves to others, who seemed better off and happier. All advanced societies are competitive by nature, since a competitive culture is how one increases wealth, power and advancement, which means individuals are also competitive and thus feel the constant need to be showing each other who is better. This is particularly true in societies with a global influence such as the Roman Empire or the American Empire.

Wealth and status were broadcast in identical ways then and now. Today the most popular way to show off one's wealth is by buying a big house in a location known for wealthy residents. Roman times were no different. The Palatine Hill was known for the massive mansions of the Roman elite just as a place like Beverly Hills is known for the American elite today. Because of this competitive nature, there were, and still are, those who do not feel happy about their status. They are so caught up in the hustle and bustle of daily life that they feel they lack a purpose. This also happens to those men and women who are of such a high status that they barely need to work at all. These people also may feel they lack purpose or question the meaning of life because they have a lot of time to think.

Because of this widespread need to find purpose, ease the mind, and receive praise from peers, cult religions popped up all over the ancient world, especially the Roman Empire. There were estimated to be hundreds of cult-religion meeting places in the city of Rome alone. People joined these cult-religions to fill a wide variety of gaps in their lives. Many simply wanted to be part of a community with a shared purpose, others just wanted to socialize, and many more needed to receive news about the world around them since there was no other way to voluntarily receive news at the time.

Most of the members of these cult religions had similar demographics. The Cult of Isis was made up of mostly middle or upper-class women, the Cult of Mithras was a male-only community of mostly soldiers and merchants; and finally there was the cult style branch of Judaism that overtook the urban centers of the Roman Empire, which is now known as Christianity, and was mostly made up of wealthy members of Roman society. All of these cult-religions had initiations to impose certain values on the members, a hierarchy of membership, and meetings generally held in secret to keep information within the community[10] (See Further Readings).

With this history in mind, let us look at a wealthy and advanced nation in modern times such as the United States. Countless Americans face the same issues described above. They need to fill various gaps in their lives. Therefore, just as the Romans joined cult-like groups who had a charismatic leader they related to, Americans follow the views of charismatic people they relate to as well…on social media. Just as many Romans got the majority of their information from religious leaders they chose to follow for news, opinions, and perspectives on others, Americans today get the majority of their news, opinions and perspectives from those they follow on social media.

However, there is one significant societal issue with both cult religions and social media that greatly impacted Romans and has already impacted Americans. This issue is the matter of filtered information. Whoever one follows (either in religion or social media) effectively becomes a filter of information. Any information that this "leader" receives or creates is filtered, edited, and subject to opinion when he transmits it to his followers. This can be either deliberate or unconscious, but no matter what the reasoning, information transmitted through selected filters ultimately leads to inaccurate information, and consequently, TIP among communities of all sizes.

In other words, individuals only follow those who share their beliefs and thus only hear what they want to believe. Romans joined cult religions that had values with which they could agree. They only joined cults that told them what they wanted to hear and thus received extremely limited information about the world around them because they received almost all their information from these cult leaders who they chose to follow in the first place. Likewise, Americans typically only follow accounts that make them happy, or give them information they agree with. A Republican will probably not follow a Democratic speaker on Twitter and the outspoken Democrat will probably not follow a far-right Republican speaker.

Although we can easily see the reasoning behind this human flaw to filter information to that which runs alongside our values or simply makes us happy, this can become extremely dangerous when it starts to happen on all levels of society. When communities of people are only hearing things that reinforce the values they already have, new ideas begin to taper off, communities begin to lose inter-community connections, and overall societal progress slows to a halt. When huge numbers of people are only receiving information through a filter that they have deliberately chosen, it becomes unbelievably easy for entire populations to quickly become misinformed.

For any society, its citizens must understand alternate perspectives; this is absolutely essential, and this is done through genuine connections and as many of them as possible. Again, interconnectivity is key to maintaining high levels of CSW and ensuring societal progress. Let's consider two examples of how misinformation due to the Tragedy of Isolated

Perspective leads to the decompensation of both societies at play.

Say there is a plot of land between two groups of people: Group A and Group B. Group A has a growing population that needs jobs so they want to work the land for any job available. Group B is more of a management type and wants to use the land to build more factories and expand their business. Group A has more desperate needs, so they decide to move into the land and set up small markets to sell little toys and trinkets that they can make with local resources.

Without interconnectivity, Group B simply sees Group A moving into the land Group B was going to use to build their factories so Group B immediately moves into the land and starts building their factories where Group A's markets reside to prevent Group A from taking over all the land. Group A exclaims, "Nobody agreed that you could use this land for your factories!" and Group B says, "Well nobody agreed that you could move into the land in the first place for your markets!"

Now that tensions have begun to rise, Group A, the merchants, thinks that Group B. the factory owners, is out to get them since as soon as they moved into the open land, Group B came in to try to kick them out. Group B thinks Group A is a bunch of sneaky cheaters who jumped on the free land before any agreement was made.

This is the Tragedy of Isolated Perspective. Neither group thought to try and understand why the other was making the actions they were making. Neither group decides to give up their position so both stay. Then Tragedy of the Commons sets in. The factories are less productive because the small markets are in their way, and the markets are less productive because the factories are polluting the air and ruining the land. Consequently, Group B is spending more money and resources to fund their new inefficient factories and Group A is going out of their way to set up more and more markets around the factory which drives down prices to their own products. Both groups are worse off than before. The lack of interconnectivity and consequential lack of CSW led to a societal regression for both communities.

Let us now analyze a real-world situation:

Say there is a plot of land that Group MEX lives on that happens to be adjacent to a community called Group USA. Let's call this plot of land Mexico. Group MEX are the residents of Mexico and Group USA are the residents of an adjacent plot of land called the United States. Group MEX has a growing population that need jobs, so they want to work the land for any available job. Group USA wants to use the land to build more factories and expand their business.

Let's say that this time both groups did make a deal. Group MEX, the Mexicans, said they will allow Group USA to build their factories on their land if Group MEX could work in them. Thus, members of Group MEX were employed, and Group USA built their factories and received more labor. However, since Group MEX's population is growing so fast, jobs are running out and people are offering to work for less and less wages. Group USA, the Americans, notices this and decides it would be way more cost-effective to move all their factories in America to the land of Group MEX, or Mexico, for cheaper labor.

So now factories are popping up left and right in Group MEX's land and Group USA's domestic factories are all getting torn down. However, Group MEX, the residents of Mexico, thinks that Group USA, the Americans, is deliberately lowering wages while simultaneously taking over their land because the members of Group MEX do not actually know the reasoning for Group USA's actions. Meanwhile, the Americans, or Group USA, have suddenly had a large number of their jobs taken away because their own domestic factories have been moved to Mexico. The Americans now think the Mexicans are deliberately stealing their jobs. Tensions rise.

Group MEX, the Mexicans, gets so angry because of their dirt-cheap wages that they decide to boycott working for Group USA's factories. The massive influx of migrants, and the low wages because of the influx of workers, keep the factory-workers in poverty despite working long hours. On the other hand, Group USA gets so angry because Group MEX has "stolen" all their jobs and now Group MEX is boycotting all their factories. Hence the American-owned factories in Mexico have to stop running due to the boycotts and are thus losing money. Consequently, the Americans start claiming that if the factories came back to America, the Americans would work them and they would all get their jobs back. Unfortunately, because of their recent investments into building all these new factories in Mexico, the Americans don't have enough money to move the factories back to the US.

So both groups have been utterly defeated by not making efforts to understand the perspectives of the other community or even attempting to work out a deal. What's worse is that both groups are now furious with each other and will refuse to work together to find a solution.

In other words, this has become another perfect example of the Tragedy of Isolated Perspective.

How does one combat the Tragedy of Isolated Perspective? Interconnectivity and education. If these two groups could put aside their emotions and preconceived notions about the other group, they could meet and hold a productive conversation to help each group better understand the feelings and needs of the other. In almost all cases, the cost of a solution that would improve both parties, even just by small increments, is much less than people usually think.

In the case of the Group Mex and Group USA quarrel, all that would need to happen to start rebuilding relationships and improving the lives of both parties would be to hold a meeting during which each party is heard and understood.

In this meeting, the Mexicans could explain that they are furious with receiving minimal wages, which is why they feel it is no longer worth it to work in the factories. The Americans could explain that they feel that the Mexicans are taking all their jobs because the factories have all moved to Mexico.

Because of the fast-growing population of Mexican workers, they end up competing with each other for jobs, which is how wages get lowered. The Americans could make a compromise to pay the Mexican workers a minimum wage, hopefully more than they are currently getting paid, to keep the workers in the factories. The new workers will eventually find new factories as more of them are opened in Mexico.

The Americans who need jobs will also need some guarantees for their careers. Take the American factory workers. They are feeling that they no longer have jobs because the factories moved to Mexico.

Many of these workers are highly experienced. Some of them might even have ways to improve factory work so that it is more efficient or safe or better in some way. Say for example that some workers believe factories should be ran a certain way with a certain improved safety feature. There is nothing stopping these workers from getting together and starting a new business to build and sell this new safety product. They could then sell this product to the Mexican factories, thus making themselves money, and making the Mexican workers safer. Some of these Americans could even be hired as consultants and teach the management and workers in these new Mexican factories how they could be run most efficiently. Additionally, a deal could be cut which would allow the experienced factory workers to act as consultants for new factories, therefore still maintaining a career in the field they are familiar with.

In other words, if people use a bit of creativity, they will always find ways to use their skills in a way which is helpful and profitable. Additionally, there is this unfounded theory in America that the job market is like a pie where everybody gets a piece of the pie and if there is none left, you're out of luck. This is a false notion. There are always fields where jobs are growing and new areas of growth in the job market. And furthermore, in the US you can practically start a business for free at any moment. One must simply be willing to adapt and build some skills he may not be fully familiar with if he wants to find employment. In the Age of Information, employees must be constantly growing their skillsets, because if they are not, they will be left behind by the ones who are.

With regard to the US and Mexico example, the issues at stake are obviously much more complex in the real world than what is described here. However, the point is that there must be constant quality human connections between communities to exchange information, ideas, emotions, and opinions. Otherwise the Tragedy of Isolated Perspective can take place, which can, and almost always will, negatively affect both parties.

Fear: The Ultimate Cause of the Loss of Interconnectivity

We have now discussed the importance of interconnectivity to all societies large and small, especially regarding a nation's Collective Societal Wisdom. I further hope that I have made it abundantly clear that preventing the decline of interconnectivity is not only important, but vital to a community's long-term welfare.

I have described how CSW shapes societies and how interconnectivity effects CSW. Now it is time to discuss the root cause of declining interconnectivity and the consequential decline in Collective Societal Wisdom. That cause is fear. The idea of fear seems simple. Fear is one of the most instinctual, most reflexive, and most powerful emotions of any complex being. Fear is vital to life but also extraordinarily dangerous if left uncontrolled. Despite being one of the most recognizable emotions, fear, and its effects on the mind, are not widely discussed among the general population.

Fear is, and always has been, the single greatest threat to the welfare of any society in any part of the world at any time. The reason for this is the paralyzing nature of fear with regards to the mind. By design, fear is meant to be a reflex, an instinctual reaction to the perception of danger. Because of this, fear blinds the mind to rational thinking. Logic and reason become inactive. Hence, systemic fear permeating an entire population can eliminate rational thinking so swiftly and on such a widespread, collective level that entire societies can make poor decisions that put themselves in extraordinarily dangerous situations, which would otherwise seem totally unbelievable to a rational mind.

One might ask how can a whole population become so afraid? The answer is quite simple. People are afraid of what they do not understand. When a community collectively does not understand a wide range of things regarding themselves and the world around them, they replace this misunderstanding with the natural reflex known as fear. When people become afraid, they revert only to things they are familiar with and fully understand and consequently their knowledge, experiences and perspectives plateau.

Here are some definitions of the word fear:

i.　　Merriam-Webster definition of fear: "an unpleasant often strong emotion caused by anticipation or awareness of danger"

ii.　　Cambridge definition of fear: "a strong emotion caused by great worry about something dangerous, painful, or unknown that is happening or might happen"

iii.　　Oxford English dictionary definition of fear: "An unpleasant emotion caused by the threat of danger, pain, or harm.

Each of these definitions have one thing in common: the *perception* of the *unknown*. We can see that the words used in these definitions, "anticipation," "great worry," and "threat," all have to do with perception. Thus, fear is almost exclusively caused by one's interpretation of what they do not understand.

In other words, fear is simply a mental reaction to the unknown.

This idea is reflected in the countless phobias that people experience on a day-to-day basis. When asked why those who fear spiders are afraid of spiders, they generally cannot give a solid answer. This is because they do not inherently know exactly why they fear spiders. As we know, it is the fear of what *might* happen with the spider, not knowing where it will crawl or if it will bite or not, which triggers the reaction of mind-numbing fear.

One of the most profound fears that has arisen in the modern era is the crisis of unemployment fears in America. Every child is told from a very young age that they "must be able to get a good job," or "if they do this, they won't be able to get a good job." This ideology translates into young people only doing what they "know" can get them a job, which of course is to become what the corporations want them to become. Corporations market themselves as providing "job security" for their workers which leads young people to only learn what the corporations ask them to learn during that time period.

Unfortunately, this leads to increasing specialization – as a corporation runs into an issue in a certain area or discovers growth in another, they will broadcast this quite clearly to the young members of society, especially at universities. However, the increase in specialization across fields in Western civilization has one significant consequence. Those who specialize further and further tend to start lacking or disregarding other areas of knowledge. As we know from previous chapters, innovation stems from the merging of two or more fields of knowledge. Therefore, if everybody starts to only focus on one specific area, innovation becomes hindered.

I briefly touched on the importance of innovation in the earlier chapter on the causes of declining CSW and most educated folk agree that innovation is a key piece to macro-scale progress. However, many still fail to see the ways in which innovation is stimulated. As explained earlier, innovation is simply a fancy term for creation. But creation does not simply appear out of nowhere. Creation stems from the mixing and matching of ideas from various perspectives and areas of knowledge.

Businesses have figured out that innovation is boosted if their workplaces are designed to be a "creative environment." But what exactly is a creative environment? An image of a San Francisco startup office may come to mind with lots of bright colors, and medicine-ball chairs and a slide in the middle of the office. There may be some truth in saying that this type of environment may stimulate more creativity than a classic whitewashed floor full of cubicles. But the reasons for this are not directly because of the sensory stimulations within the environment or the fact that there are beds in the breakroom.

Innovation is the merging of two or more fields. All ideas are built upon other ideas and new creations always stem from old creations. Therefore, true progress is built by combining different pieces of knowledge and different perspectives. Thus, work environments that stimulate creativity are environments which promote interconnectivity among workers in different departments with different knowledgebases and perspectives.

On a larger scale, the increasing trend economy-wide toward specialization can actually stifle innovation. This is because increasing individual specialization requires constantly increasing effort spent to keep up with that single field of study or area of work. When researchers or laborers are taught to specialize in increasingly narrow fields, the pressure to produce quality results falls on the individual, rather than the community or company or nation as a whole. This individualistic culture prevents persons within a population from wanting to "waste their time" on other "irrelevant" knowledge-bases which, in turn, prevents connections from being built and thus smothers the flow of knowledge and ideas, and consequently, innovation.

If a patient comes to a doctor because of a heart problem, they may see a cardiologist. However, we know that the human body is a vastly complex system, and each part is connected in a multitude of ways, influencing, and being influenced by, other parts of the body. For example, a heart problem could stem from something as simple as a poor diet. Although this person may be seeing the world's best cardiologist who may know exactly what is wrong within the heart, this cardiologist may not be a diet specialist. So although the cardiologist could diagnose the heart problem with perfect precision and could provide medication to treat the problem (which would bring side effects of course and not treat the cause in the first place), he may not have the knowledge of how the patient could alleviate the heart issue by changing their diet in a certain way.

However, if the cardiologist had enough of a broader knowledge base, he may be able to tell the patient about the diet as well. Or at the very least, if the cardiologist did not only spend time with other cardiologists, he may be able to refer the patient to an outside doctor who has a better knowledge of nutrition and its effects on the body.

Note that I am not explicitly saying that specialization is wrong or dangerous outright, but that those who specialize in exceptionally narrow fields must be careful not to get caught up in a pool of the same recycled knowledge and perspectives. They must take steps to broaden their knowledge and remain open to outside ideas and perceptions. Entities of all scales must remember that true innovation comes from the merging of two or more fields.

Businesses also must understand that the lack of integration between fields actually produces less productive businesses. Building assembly line corporations where each employee has one job and if anything falls outside of their job description, they either ignore it or pass it on to their boss, prevents employees from reaching their full productive potential. This phenomenon has led to increased stress and workload of managers who are thus constantly putting out fires rather than spending time building a better business.

However, a company with well-rounded employees who have easy access to coworkers in other departments in order to exchange ideas or ask for help will be significantly more profitable. As is the theme throughout this book, expanding channels for communication and connection leads to increasing productivity, innovation, and knowledge, and the more knowledge that is passed on, the less fear there will be.

Overall, the fear of unemployment or even the fear of "losing the edge" in business has caused society to move towards increasing specialization, thus decreasing the amount of exchange of ideas and knowledge "outside the field."

The mental reaction of the unknown, otherwise known as fear, is a powerful reflex shared by every human around the globe. By understanding that fear stems from the unknown or misunderstood, we must do everything in our power to maintain channels of communication between different communities. Furthermore, when communities or individual are afraid, they must take great care to ensure they do not close down and isolate themselves, which would cut off their channels of outside information, thus leading to further misinformation and misunderstanding. The following chapter will describe in detail how fear has affected the US border crisis and the opinions surrounding the crisis.

When You Are Afraid, Strengthen Your Borders?

In psychology, there is a common phenomenon in people who have experienced emotional trauma and have become terrified of reliving that trauma and therefore close themselves off to most others and rarely open up to any sort of emotional conversation that may involve their fears. This is known as detachment and these people are usually said to have "put up walls." This defensive reaction towards fearful thinking happens identically with entire societies.

Throughout the entirety of civilization, one of the most common, and potentially dangerous, societal crises that can occur has to do with borders. Border disputes as small as that of a farm, all the way up to national borders, can have long-lasting implications, including the worst of all, war, if the crisis is not managed properly.

As almost every American knows, the United States has been having a border crisis for some time. This particular issue is not a dispute over what the border should be geographically but rather how permeable the border should be regarding migration and trade.

Just as with many border crises before, the American border crisis has become one of the most widely publicized national issues in the US. No matter where one is from, everybody has extremely strong ties to the place they call home. This is why border crises can get out of hand so quickly. And the United States is no different. As you know, many Americans have incredibly strong opinions regarding the current border crisis.

Because the general population usually has extremely adamant feelings about how the border dispute should be taken care of, politicians are put under enormous pressure. First, the solutions that the general public commonly agree upon are almost never plausible or helpful in anyway simply because, when it comes to location-based disputes, each side will almost never choose to look at the other side's perspective. They justify this by using the umbrella statement, "This is our home!" Most politicians know they must not implement the population's solution as it would probably not solve the problem.

However, if the politicians go against the general population, they risk losing voters, and possibly their jobs. because the civilians will see that the politicians went against their desires.

Hence, the policymakers are caught in a dilemma between keeping their jobs in the short term and risking long-term well-being or risking their jobs to protect long-term welfare of the state. Unfortunately, most politicians, being human with their number one priority being to protect the welfare of themselves and their families, choose to protect their own short-term well-being in order to please their constituents.

Even more important than pleasing the general population however is the nature of fear. With regards to the United States/Mexico border crisis, as well as many other border disputes based around migrant policy, both the public, and the policymakers who strive for closed borders, do so out of fear. As explained in the previous chapter, this fear arises from the uncertainty about what might happen if these new migrants enter the nation. Because of the lack of understanding which stems from a lack of interconnectivity between the two peoples, many Americans are afraid to allow the Mexican people into their nation. They are afraid of crime, they are afraid of losing their jobs, they are afraid of losing their culture. This fear all goes back to the misunderstanding that stems from the lack of interconnectivity.

Similar situations have been occurring around the world over the last decade in response to the refugee crisis stemming from the Syrian war. Many European nations have been struggling to come up with fair policies for the refugees arriving at their doorsteps.

Of course, policymaking is difficult and there is rarely a perfect solution. However, the theme of this book has been to welcome new people, cultures, and ideas with open arms in order to gain a better mutual understanding of one another so I'm sure you can guess what the solution I would suggest may be. The first and most important step in solving border disputes is to communicate, build compassion and understanding, and welcome openness. Make connections between populations, find out what each population wants and what their fears are. Work with each other rather than only deliberate with your own people. If these steps are not taken, drastic measures can and will occur.

The Roman/Gothic Border Crisis is a particular historical example that that is relevant to border permeability issues and reveals the severe consequences of mishandling immigrants or refugees. This example is almost identical to the US/Mexico border crisis and Europe/Syrian refugee crises, which makes it essential to study closely, allowing us to avoid the same mistakes that were made then. It happened so long ago that we can see each step that was taken and the short and long-term consequences of these steps on both populations.

The year was 376 AD. The Roman Empire had recently suffered major economic setbacks causing many changes in policy in order to save costs and keep the taxpayers happy. To the East, the Huns had arrived, causing mass death and destruction, forcing many populations outside of the Empire, such as the Goths, to flee their homes and rush to the Roman Empire, which boasted the most powerful military in the world, where they knew their families could be protected. The Goths were so afraid of what was happening in their homeland that they were willing to risk moving to a new, vastly different nation, and potentially losing their culture and traditions that their ancestors had known for so long.

Eventually, word reached the ears of the Roman Emperor Valens that over 100,000 Goths, mainly women and children, were camped outside the Roman border on the far side of the Danube River. The Goths were asking for permission to settle within the Roman borders since their homes were all destroyed. They would submit to Roman rule and pay Roman taxes in order to have Roman protection. Emperor Valens agreed to allow them into the borders but disregarded the fact that all these people would need land allocated, food provided, and some money in order to start their lives from scratch again.

The local Romans on the other hand quickly became furious at this influx of foreigners. The local administrations first attempted to limit the number of Goths who were allowed to enter Roman lands, and then refused to give any sort of aid to those who had already crossed. Therefore, months went by with the Goths living within Roman borders in filthy refugee camps, sickly and starving. Some Goths were said to have been forced to sell their children into slavery to Roman authorities in exchange for meat. The Roman historian who detailed these events, Ammianus Marcellinus, wrote that because the Goths, "Were not supplied the necessaries of life…they were being forced to disloyalty as a remedy for the evils that threatened them" (Marcellinus).

The Goths could only take this mistreatment for so long and eventually began raiding the Roman countryside for food and supplies. Upon hearing this, Emperor Valens made one of the most substantial blunders in the history of Rome and decided to march an imperial army against the Goths. This decision resulted in the Battle of Adrianople in 378 where the desperate, starving Goths defeated the Roman legion and killed Emperor Valens. The Romans were so utterly baffled by this turn of events that they were forced to negotiate peace terms with the Goths, essentially giving the Goths direct control of the land they occupied. Many modern historians list this event as one of the key events that triggered the total collapse of the Roman Empire.

Let's take a step back and analyze the Roman/Goth border crisis. The main issue that first arose was that the ordinary Roman citizens became furious that the Goths were crossing into their land. Try to imagine yourself as a Roman local in that situation. Why might you be angry? The Goths were not taking anybody's land or resources, they were simply staying in camps directly on the border. But the local Romans were still angry. The most logical conclusion is that the Romans were actually afraid. They were afraid because they did not know why the Goths were there, and did not know what the Goths were going to do. Furthermore, they did not understand Gothic culture, which consisted of different clothes, language, and other visible cultural aspects.

In the minds of the Romans, the Goths had just brought thousands of their people into Roman land for absolutely no reason. The Romans did not understand that the homeland of these people had been razed to the ground. Furthermore, the Romans did not understand that the Goths were simply trying to survive.

The Goths, on the other hand, were absolutely terrified as well. They were afraid for their safety. They were afraid of the warlike Romans who were avoiding them at all costs. The Goths also had been given no idea as to how long they would have to remain starving in the camps, or whether they would be able to integrate into Roman society at all.

It was a classic case of the Tragedy of Isolated Perspective. Because of the language barrier, the Goths and Romans could hardly communicate with each other. Because of the difference in cultural traditions, both groups thought the other was acting strangely. As time went by, suspicions within each community about the other grew. All the while the Goths were starving, and the Romans refused to help. It is thus no surprise that eventually the Goths had to take survival into their own hands.

Hence, the Roman fears that the Goths were looting criminals who were there to steal the Romans' land swiftly became a self-fulfilling prophecy. If the Romans had only tried to connect with the Goths in order to understand their perspectives and reason for being there, the entire issue could have been resolved before it even began. Imagine if the Romans had employed the Goths. The Roman farm and manufacturing productivity would have skyrocketed with the addition of 100,000 workers desperately in need of a job to buy food. Furthermore, if the 100,000 Goths had been granted resident status, they could have been taxed. There is no doubt that taxes from 100,000 new members of society would boost the economy in the local area, as well as the Empire as a whole. But unfortunately, the Tragedy of Isolated Perspective took over, leaving both parties worse off all because of the failure to communicate and understand the other's perspectives.

The battle of Adrianople, along with the previous hatred from the Roman people, resulted in hugely increased tensions between the Romans and the Goths for the remainder of the Roman era. In fact, it was this same group of Goths, known as the Visigoths, who ended up invading Italy and sacking the city of Rome itself only thirty-two years later, resulting in the official collapse of the Roman Empire.

The Romans learned too late the consequences of creating an enemy with one's neighbors, particularly those who have a large population within one's own borders. The United States needs to be equally wary. According to the US Census Bureau, just under one-in-five Americans are Hispanic (United States Census Bureau, 2018). With education, time, and money, Hispanics will have power, despite the deliberate efforts of some folk to prevent them from obtaining these resources. Therefore, it would be inexplicably unwise for the conservative Americans to continue to build up hatred and tensions between themselves and the Hispanics. Creating an enemy within one's own border is not only dangerous but will always lead to problems down the road for both groups of people. In the case of the Roman and Gothic peoples, the hosts of the land were hit the hardest.

However, returning to the problem of the fear of the Roman people and the lack of understanding between the Romans and the Goths, we can use this example to determine where the problems began and how to solve them in parallel situations within the modern world. This is exceptionally important for the US/Mexico border crisis and the Syrian diaspora of refugees in Europe and the Middle East as the Roman/Gothic border crisis had almost identical beginnings and the reactions of both parties were identical as well.

Because this book focuses on the United States, I will go into detail regarding the US/Mexico border crisis. However, note that nearly identical reactions are present in the Syrian refugee crisis as well. We know from the Rome/Goth crisis that the Romans were afraid of the Goths coming into their land for two reasons.

The first was that the Romans simply did not know why they were coming. And because of the differences in culture, the Romans assumed that the Goths were 'outsiders' and 'barbarians.' All the Roman people knew about barbarians was what the government officials had told them: that barbarians were savages and criminals. These statements terrified the Romans as nobody wanted criminals and savages in their land.

The Romans were also afraid because they felt that their own culture was being threatened since the culture and traditions of the Goths and Romans were drastically different. For example, the Goths wore beards; the Romans were cleanly shaven. The Gothic men wore pants, the Romans did not, as they believed it was manly to show off one's legs. The Goths had different religious beliefs than the Romans. The Goths lived in wooden huts, the Romans built with brick and stone. However, these differences were all arbitrary. It was not truly these differences that built hatred between the peoples but rather the perception of what these differences meant.

With regard to the United States and Mexico, the Americans who feel that Hispanic immigrants should not be allowed into the country are ultimately afraid. And these Americans are afraid in the exact same ways the Romans feared the Gothic immigrants. Many Americans have been told by misinformed folk that Hispanic people are 'savages' or 'criminals.' Many Americans are afraid that the influx of a new culture will change their own longstanding culture and traditions. Many Americans are afraid they will lose their land or their jobs. This is identical to the attitudes of the ancient Romans.

However, in the same way that the Gothic people were simply looking for security and opportunity, that is exactly what the Hispanic immigrants are looking for. Finally, due to the difference in language, understanding one another is even more difficult, which leads to fewer connections and more suspicions.

Regrettably, it seems in the current time that many Americans are falling into the same mindsets and mistakes that the Romans found themselves in. They are avoiding any interaction with these new people, may of which who are not even new to the nation, and are refusing to try to understand why they are here and what they want. Instead, many Americans against immigration are isolating themselves with what they think they know, which then kickstarts the Tragedy of Isolated Perspective.

Moreover, not only are these Americans building up hatred and isolating themselves, but they are completely failing to see the opportunities that can arise from an influx of people. For example, there has been extensive talk about the feasibility of social security in the United States. It has been calculated that social security will eventually run out of money. This is because the Baby Boomer generation is so large, and they have almost all entered retirement. Furthermore, with the explosion in new medical technology, people are living longer and thus receive social security payments for many more years. Additionally, population growth in the US has nearly plateaued which means not as many new people are entering the workforce to pay taxes over the long term. So how can the US add more money into the social security system without individuals paying more taxes?

Well, imagine if all the immigrants in the US were granted citizenship. This would mean they can get jobs, boosting economic output, but also, this would mean they can be taxed for social security and other taxes. The Pew Research Center estimated that there were 10.7 million undocumented immigrants living in the US in 2016 (López, Bialik, & Radford, 2018). Imagine if almost 11 million people suddenly became documented, bringing them under the tax umbrella. This would be a huge amount of income for the American government, which could be reflected in social programs such as social security.

Throughout history, fear has led to hate, and hate has led to isolation. Another example of this occurred during the first few centuries of a religion quite familiar to much of the world: Christianity. It is broadly known that Christianity was a small offshoot of a widespread religion within the Middle East, Judaism. In fact, there are no records that show the followers of Christ actually referring to themselves as Christian until centuries after his lifetime. They simply believed they were another sect of Judaism. Additionally, the entire world around them, which was controlled by none other than the Roman Empire, simply saw them as just another sect of Judaism as well. That was true until the Christians began to break some very old Jewish traditions.

Despite what most Christians believe today, the Romans were incredibly tolerant of religions other than their own. The most probable reason for this was that the extent of the Roman Empire encompassed so many different religions that it would be much more politically profitable to simply allow people to practice whatever religion they pleased, rather than try to control all of them. In fact, the Romans sometimes enjoyed other faiths so much that they adopted many aspects of other religions and incorporated them into their own traditions just as other religions, such as Christianity, adopted pagan rituals and traditions as well.

One such example of this occurred in the later Roman Empire when Christianity was becoming mainstream. Christians in the Roman Empire enjoyed the ancient Roman winter festival known as Saturnalia so much so that they adopted the festival into Christianity. The centuries-old Saturnalia festival, which would begin on December 17, was a time of celebration, gift-giving, decorating, and honoring those who are of lesser status. Even when Christians started banning pagan holidays and traditions, the influence of the Saturnalia festival was so large that they converted it into a Christian holy day, or holiday.

One of the most significant troubles with honoring Jesus Christ in early Christianity was that Christ's actual date of birth was not recorded in the bible. Hence, a decision was made by the Christians in power to simply move the celebration of Jesus Christ's birthday to the widely celebrated birthday of the Roman sun-god, Solis Invicti or "Invincible Sun," which occurred on December 25th just after the official end of Saturnalia. This day of course is still celebrated as the birth of Jesus today.

Many religions in the ancient world intersected with each other and traded traditions that became quite significant. However, as most Westerners know, the tolerance and respect between the Romans and Christians did not last. As stated above, for many decades, and even centuries, the Romans and Christians did not identify that the Christians were anything different than the followers of the ancient Jewish faith. They worshipped the same god, they utilized the same text and stories, and they even lived in the same geographic areas.

However, the Christians suddenly began to start holding meetings in secret, underground locations, and denounced their faith's title as Jewish. In fact, the Greek word "ekklesia," which was used over 100 times in the New Testament was incorrectly translated into "church" in every instance with the exception of five times, when the New Testament was translated into English (New American Standard New Testament Greek Lexicon). The real definition of "ekklesia" was to describe the elected administrative assembly that governed Athens. Thus, in the original words of the Bible itself, the early Christian meetings were simply assemblies of elected individuals.

Of course, the Romans began to wonder what exactly was going on behind closed doors. Suspicions were heightened further when the Romans heard word that the Christians were consuming the body and blood of a man whom they did not know. To the Romans, these rumors sounded horrifically similar to cannibalism. This tradition of course became known as the eucharist. Then, the Romans began to discover that these Christians were refusing to make sacrifices to the Roman gods, as all Roman citizens were supposed to do. This was a great insult to the Roman gods and of course to the hugely superstitious Romans themselves who believed that insulting the gods could lead to absolute disaster for all.

Finally, all these suspicions quickly became persecution. Here we see the issues of fear-driven perspectives coming into play. The Romans were generally extremely tolerant of other religions and traditions. However, the Christians feared the Romans and therefore isolated themselves by meeting behind closed doors. The Romans then began to fear what was going on behind those closed doors, and the entire situation became a vicious cycle.

This becomes another example of the Tragedy of Isolated Perspective. Fear begets isolation, which then prevents both sides from understanding one another. This leads to more fear and more isolation. As we know, isolation leads to fewer connections and thus less understanding between communities, which ultimately causes diminishing Collective Societal Wisdom.

Because fear so quickly leads to blaming, we must take great efforts to attempt to understand what we are afraid of and why we are afraid. As the great Stoic philosopher Epictetus stated 2000 years ago, "Small-minded people habitually reproach others for their own misfortunes. Average people reproach themselves. Those who are dedicated to a life of wisdom understand that to blame something or someone is foolishness, that there is nothing to be gained in blaming, whether it be others or oneself" (Epictetus, 1994).

Roman Collapse: How the Roman Empire collapsed twice, ultimately descending into the Dark Ages

Now that we have an idea as to how fear causes a series of reactions which leads to decreasing CSW, we can look at how these factors played out for the Roman Empire. As we know, the Roman Empire is striking not only because of its wealth, power, prestige, influence, and longevity; it is equally renowned for its famous collapse. In fact, Roman society experienced total political collapse not once, but twice.

The first collapse of Roman society was the rather violent 'transition' from the Roman Republic to the Roman Empire. Interestingly, this occurred around 100 years after the multi-generational cold-war, and eventual physical war, with the competing world power in the Mediterranean, the Carthaginian Empire. Some historians have compared the aftermath of the Roman victory over Carthage in 146 BC with the American-proclaimed "victory" over the Soviet Union after the Soviet collapse.

However, the more captivating aspect of the collapse of the Roman Republic is the fact that after all the chaos, the nation resorted to giving up freedoms in exchange for an authoritarian figure. After the dust settled from the Republic's collapse, the Roman nation was transformed into an imperial system, with a single man controlling the kingdom with *imperium*, the Latin term that essentially translates to 'the power to command [military forces]."

This of course is nothing unfamiliar. Authoritarians taking control of entire nations after a time of chaos has consistently occurred throughout the history of civilization. But the scary part is that none of these populations knew that this was occurring during the time of 'transition.' The general population was completely unaware of the fact that they were giving up their freedoms. Hence, before I discuss the total collapse of the Roman Empire and descent into the Dark Ages, I want to briefly outline some visible factors that occur after times of chaos when societies are teetering on the edge of authoritarian takeover.

The first, but not necessarily the easiest, sign to spot is income inequality within a population. Drastic income inequality leaves the masses unhappy and with nothing to lose, a dangerous combination. Strangely, income inequality generally becomes visible with massive amounts of wealth being spent publicly by the upper class. In ancient civilizations, especially Rome, this wealth came to the surface in the form of monumental construction projects, which cost exorbitant amounts of money and always had the patron's name attached to them.

This type of massive, publicly-visible spending is identical to that of the oligarchs in the modern world as well. Foundations and organizations, buildings, donations, and many other name-based entities are formed by the elite to increase their power and influence, while attempting to justify their vast wealth and power.

These individual-based spending sprees in the public eye are a blatant sign of significant income-inequality in a nation, which means a society is vulnerable to an authoritarian transition.

Another obvious sign of vulnerability to an authoritarian takeover, which runs hand-in-hand with income inequality is bureaucratic expansion. The volume and speed of small business being absorbed by large businesses is a vital signal that entities are being compiled into bureaucracies. Whether these bureaucracies are private or state entities does not matter. The transfer of influence, wealth, and power into the hands of the few directly eliminates the freedom of those within and around these bureaucracies.

As mega-businesses swallow up or beat small businesses in unfair competitions, the freedom of choice for the individual citizen becomes limited. For example, around half of all dollars spent on online retail in the United States are spent through Amazon (Amazon Now Has Nearly 50% of US Ecommerce Market, 2018). Is that by consumer choice? Some say yes. And they are technically right. Nobody is forcing anybody else to buy products through Amazon. However, the logistical capabilities of Amazon put many other businesses, both large and small, out of business entirely. Therefore, the question becomes this: if there are only a handful of choices of where to take your business, is that really free choice?

It is important to remember that limiting choice of any kind on the macro scale is limiting freedom. Many allow themselves to be convinced that choices simply being present means they have free will. This is not the case. We must know when our freedoms are being limited and never compromise. Anyway, back to the Roman collapse narrative.

The second collapse of the Roman political system is what most people think of when the fall of

Rome is brought up. This is the collapse of the Roman Imperial system, which eventually brought Western Europe into the Dark Ages. The most significant, and easily measurable, aspect of the Roman Empire's collapse was the skyrocketing inflation and all its consequences.

Due to the overexpansion of the Roman military endeavors, and the costs of administration for the countless conquered territories (as well as the actual military upkeep costs themselves), the Roman government found themselves in a dire financial situation. Around 90% of Roman government revenue came from taxation of the blue-collar, subsistence farmer, 80% of which went to support the Roman military. There was no surprise that this was not sustainable. And what does the machine do when they need more money? Print more money! Or in the Roman case, mint more coins.

Beginning only a few decades after the imperial system prevailed, Roman emperors began to debase the silver denarius, the standard unit of currency for the Roman Empire. Original denarii were essentially standard units of weight for silver as each coin was made of 98% silver. However, it is suggested that Nero first debased the denarius to 93%, and emperors over the next 150 years followed suit, eventually leading to the denarius holding no value in silver at all in 269 AD, thus becoming all but worthless. Consequently, the Roman government began refusing to accept their own standard currency for taxation since the coin no longer held any value and other kingdoms refused to exchange any currency for the denarius. This explains why one Roman tax-collector in the 4th century AD wrote a letter to his brother asking for money to buy gold due to the rumor of further inflation (Elliot, 2014).

A drastic, unchecked increase in inflation rates of a nation's standard currency can have a slew of negative effects on a nation's political situation as well as that of the population itself. In fact, the United States and many other nations around the world are experiencing identical consequences to that which the Romans experienced 1800 years ago. This is important to look at because, as Theodor Mommsen, the discoverer of the double denarius, claimed, "If one wishes to know how a State is situated, one need only look at its coins; herein are reflected its fortune and misfortune, its decline and revival. This is still the case today" (Mommsen, 1996).

During the entirety of the Roman era, and for centuries after, the vast majority of the global population was subsistence farmers. These were known as the peasants, or people who had to do physical work to survive. As always, the working-class population took the brunt of the consequences during the economic decline of the later Roman Empire. Many of these farmers were forced to abandon their homes as the taxes on their farms left them with nothing left to feed themselves or their families. Thus, there arose a trend of peasants flocking to the wealthy landowners and pledging themselves to work for these wealthy patrons for minimal wages, or in some cases nothing at all, simply to have enough food to feed their family.

This of course was the precedent for the feudal system that took over much of Europe and other places such as Japan in the following centuries. However, it is important to compare the experiences of the Romans to that of many modern working-class families who live in societies where the military, for example, takes precedent over social well-being.

In fact, the flocking of working-class families to big-business to work for poverty-level wages simply to have enough food to eat is overwhelmingly present in modern Western cultures, particularly the United States. The societal elite figured this out thousands of years ago: if you starve the peasants, they'll work for free. In many cases it becomes easy to imagine that ancient societies were vastly different than the modern world and thus cases like this become difficult to see as real. However, the heart-breaking piece is that this notion is still extremely prevalent today, but most of the population is clueless to this fact since they have known no other way.

In the Roman era, this moral destruction of the working-class population was the beginning of the total societal collapse and transition into the Dark

Ages. As millions of people were thrown into voluntary slavery due to the economic situation, there became only one goal: survival. This is a stark contrast from the communal nature of a healthy society. The need for survival is individualistic and exceptionally powerful.

Hence, across the Roman Empire, the sole focus of the vast majority of the population became the survival of his or her family unit. All thought about preserving or improving the greater good of the society was forgotten. Parents began to only teach their children exactly what they needed to know to be a quality worker for whichever wealthy landowner they had pledged themselves to. Of course, this type of learning was that of labor-learning (or assembly-line learning) rather than intellectual learning. When your survival is at stake, nobody has the time or energy to hit the books. Higher education is no longer important if one is simply working to eat each day.

Because this shift in focus was happening at such a massive scale, only a few generations needed to pass by for knowledge to become worthless. For most of the world at the time, what one *knew* did not matter even the slightest. The only important factor was what one could *do* (in the field). Subsequently, as knowledge became less important, vast amounts of knowledge were literally forgotten over the generations. This led to measurable consequences such as the faltering of technological advancement.

Not only did technological advancement come to a halt, but technology actually regressed. Medieval folk lost the technology required to make roads as the Romans did and instead used and tried to maintain the Roman roads that were already in existence. Other building and infrastructure technologies were lost as well. Almost every area of science was lost in Western Europe for centuries. Even simple but important skills like the ability to read became unnecessary for the majority of individuals. In fact, the formation of the Romance Languages was a result of various populations forgetting how to speak proper Latin over time. Creative thought was largely lost, again because most of the population was simply working to survive. Overall, there was a drastic decline in Collective Societal Wisdom shortly before the end of the Roman era.

Sadly, the United States seems to be following a similar path in certain areas. A population's ability to use one's own language has been a wonderful measurement used to analyze education levels, which is an important piece of CSW. Just as the Romans began to lose the ability to speak proper Latin, Americans are also struggling with the use of their own language. A study published in 2012 by the National Center for Education Statistics discovered that only 24% of students in 8th grade could write at a proficient level. The same percentage was found for students in 12th grade. And these studies were not small. Over 24,000 8th graders and 28,000 12th graders participated in this study (National Center for Education Statistics, 2012).

This means that less than a quarter of American students can write at an adequate level. What is more unnerving however is the language reversal and regression at the societal level that has been occurring over the last decade. Let me explain:

The use of written language at a societal level has been a journey that has lasted for thousands of years. First, communities preserved information through sketches or some sort of pictures. Over time, pictures transformed into glyphs, essentially standardized images that held a specific meaning. As civilization progressed, more advanced ways of written communication were required, and thus simple images were no longer enough to convey full sentences.

Thus, the idea of a syllabary was introduced almost everywhere on Earth where there was civilization. A syllabary is like an alphabet but where each symbol represents a syllable or pronunciation stress. The most widely used syllabary in modern times is the Japanese hiragana syllabary. The ancient Mycenaean Greek Linear B syllabary is also well-known to historians. Furthermore, Egyptian hieroglyphs and Mayan glyphs hold a combination of simple glyph meanings as well as syllables.

Likewise, Chinese characters are largely glyphic but also utilize syllabary factors.

Finally, arguably the most versatile technique of written language is the alphabet. An alphabet uses each symbol to hold one specific sound. The most widely known related alphabets are the Phoenician, Greek, Latin, and English alphabets. Hebrew and modern Arabic are a few other well-known alphabets as is Braille. Alphabets allow for language to be swiftly adaptable and universally understood.

Effective communication and language skills are essential for the progress of society. If one has the most incredible idea but cannot articulate what that idea is to others, the idea cannot make the transition to reality. Additionally, effective communication skills are crucial for interconnectivity between individuals and communities. There is no doubt that interconnectivity has declined over the last few decades as the individual identity has overtaken the importance of the community identity. It is no coincidence that this decline in actual human connection is directly correlated with the decline of communication skills globally.

Just as civilization seemed to advance from simple pictures to a few written words and meaningful symbols and finally to complex written language skills, there appears to be a language reversal taking place globally. With the onset of instant messaging, social media, and other forms of swift non-personal communication techniques, individuals around the world, and even entire companies and communities, have been moving away from complex language. Sentences have gotten shorter with simpler words used. Proper punctuation has been almost entirely dropped from the majority of written communication within the Western world (with the exception of autocorrect). Interestingly, people seem to be communicating more and more with universally familiar pictures. These pictures come in the form of emojis, memes, and GIFs. The swiftness of the reversal from advanced language to simple pictures (maybe accompanied by a few simple words) is striking.

There is absolutely no question that the lack of information in the general populace, the ease with which misinformation can be spread amongst entire populations, and the consequential lack of knowledge about communities outside of one's own, has been brought about by the drastic decline in the use of advanced communication and language skills. Furthermore, the argument that "most people still know advanced language skills and just choose not to use them when talking to most people" is equally as scary. I am not sure which is worse: a population that does not have the knowledge of advanced communication skills or a population that simply chooses not to use these skills in most areas of life.

In the case of the Roman collapse into the Dark Ages and loss of information and technology, much of this knowledge and literature was thankfully preserved and built upon outside of Europe by the Islamic caliphates throughout the Middle East, North Africa, and southern Iberia. This knowledge and technology were eventually to be rediscovered in Europe with the onset of the renaissance hundreds of years later.

Another phenomenon that is extremely important to take note of when a society is going through any sort of transition is the trend of victimization. When a community of any size is going through a period of change, the individuals that make up that community are all going through the transition and making changes at differing speeds. This causes great tension between individuals and leads to a powerful desire for people to belong to the "right" groups. There will always be different subgroups of a community at different stages of accepting change. However, when a change happens upon a community, no matter the cause, it becomes difficult for people within the community to immediately find their stance on the change. Consequently, people will either jump in to 100% support the change or go 100% against the change. In other words, people are drawn to the extremes.

Within a movement towards a change in any society, there is almost always a focus group that the movement is expecting to benefit the most from change. Most of the times, these groups are disadvantaged or suffering in some way. This group is commonly known as the victims. This is the group that has struggled and are activating as many people as possible in order to better their lives. This has always been a very effective way of forwarding a group's acceptance, power, influence, and overall well-being.

However, in past societies and in the present day, a culture sometimes arises where the identification with being a victim becomes so overwhelming that individuals, and sometimes entire communities, begin to associate being a victim with their actual identity. Although there is no doubt that being a victim can certainly be a piece of one's identity, identifying oneself first as a victim, and second as whatever else they identify as can be dangerous.

A strong victim culture can be incredibly seductive for many people going through a transitional period within their life or in the society as a whole. People who feel they are not fitting in with certain groups or simply don't feel a sense of belonging at all may start looking for ways to achieve some sort of status allowing them to quickly identify as unique. This is usually not a conscious decision but rather a more subtle way in which the brain searches for ways to satisfy its relational and social needs to belong to a tribe.

One might ask, "Why is associating victim status as a significant piece of identity dangerous?"

Well, victim has inherently negative connotations and, for the most part, real victims have actually suffered terrible experiences. However, quickly jumping to the conclusion that one is a victim and consequently associating with others who solely think of themselves as a victim can lead to a community whose sole focus is to accept others as victims and remember that they themselves are victims. Furthermore, the growing trend to identify as a victim promotes helplessness as a virtue, which can be disempowering in other areas of life.

This quick acceptance of one being a victim can very quickly lead to the bystander effect about the very issue that made them a victim in the first place. If so much energy is put into promoting to one's community that her or she is a victim, less effort seems to be placed on actually advocating for change.

One such example of this was during the Women's March a couple of years ago when children were not allowed on the buses to Washington DC. Many mothers were thus not able to participate in the march unless they drove themselves, which does not represent a very supportive community. A significant part of the Women's March was to bring awareness to women's rights issues, particularly for mothers, such as maternity leave being too short, childcare being too expensive, breastfeeding not being acceptable in certain places, and all the other countless issues women in the US face daily. All these women were participating in the march to advocate for these issues but some seemed to be so focused on the issues themselves that they forgot to think about the changes they could make, starting amongst themselves.

The alternative issue with strongly associating being a victim with one's identity is that it creates an Us vs. Them mentality. As we know from our knowledge about the Tragedy of Isolated Perspective, Us vs. Them mentalities among communities always leads to blaming. When the focus of a community transfers from cooperation with other groups, to blaming other groups, the movement that was trying to advocate for the victims in the first place ends up sparking more divisiveness between communities rather than building rapport.

Communities that make statements such as, "They'll never understand us because they haven't been through what we have," sparks the same effect as communities saying, "Those immigrants will never understand us because they don't speak our language," or wealthy folk saying, "The working-class will never understand everything we have to go through as wealthy, powerful people."

These types of statements are extremely dangerous and end up being more divisive than if nothing had been done in the first place. Furthermore, the selfishness and isolationist undertones of Us vs. Them within these statements can actually hinder change rather than promote it. As I explained earlier in the book, the trend from "How can I help others," to "How can others help me" is a subtle change in perspective but with drastic consequences. If the entire world started saying, "How can others help me," suddenly nobody would be helping anybody.

Of course, in the late Roman world, that exact thing happened. So many communities began blaming one another for their problems rather than working together on how to stimulate change that could benefit all. Consequently, these quarrels split the people apart, until the whole Western world lost so much Collective Societal Wisdom that they ultimately collapsed into the Dark Ages, where the focus was on the smallest possible societal unit, the individual and his or her family. But if families are not working together with other families, even those with different experiences, it will be drastically more difficult to stimulate change that could make everybody better off. In the case of the Romans, when people stopped cooperating and instead started blaming, people of every social class suffered.

PART III

Solutions

What the Romans Missed

-

Solutions for the Present

We can all see the essentiality of strong Collective Societal Wisdom in any society and the importance that interconnectivity plays in a society's CSW. We know that fear is the most dangerous force to maintaining a growing level of CSW, which means fear is the most significant threat to the well-being and longevity of a society. Fear leads to isolationism, which causes a long-term decrease in CSW. We have seen how allowing fear get out of hand can drastically impact massive, sophisticated, powerful, and even well-educated societies such as the Roman or American Empires.

So, the final question is this: What is a solution that can counter every instance of fear among a community, even one as large as the United

States, or the world for that matter? What is the one area of focus that everybody, no matter how different we are, should be participating in, with at least a portion of our efforts? What could the Romans have done to prevent dragging the entire world into the Dark Ages?

The answer is quite simple, but the question of how to get there is not. The answer is this: extensive, fully accessible, and high-quality education of the *entire population*.

Education is the solution to fear. As we know, fear is the brain's interpretation of what one does not know or fully understand. Education provides knowledge, understanding, and alternate perspectives. Therefore, all-encompassing education is the direct solution to fear, even fears that may arise in the future. A desire for greater understanding of knowledge and perspectives will help counteract fears that can be blown out of proportion in the present, and in the future.

The Pew Research Center found that there is a direct correlation between education and positive views on increasing diversity (Poushter, Fetterolf, & Tamir, 2019). If we know that diversity increases the exchange of knowledge, ideas, and perspectives, then we must provide stronger education for the next generations so that they desire more diversity and thus more education, and it becomes a cycle.

Of course, many Americans would argue that we already have "widespread" education "for all." The Romans would have argued the same. In fact, in the Roman era, their education was quite similar to that of the United States and much of the modern Western world. The Romans had the equivalent of grade school in their time. They were taught basic knowledge that was necessary to function in daily life such as reading, writing and simple arithmetic (Parkin & Pomeroy, 2007). However, this type of education lacked any sort of teachings about perspectives and how one can think about the effects of other perspectives on him or herself, in addition to that of his perspective on others.

Just like in much of the developed world, many citizens back then knew that this basic education was not enough. In the Roman era, students would seek out a teacher for more advanced learning such as rhetoric in order to expand their minds further. However, to find highly experienced and knowledgeable teachers, students would have to attend the large institutions, generally in major cities. This of course costs significant amounts of time and money.

In fact, this system too was quite similar to the education system in the Western world. Many of us know that a simple grade school education will not suffice in providing our minds with the greatest tools to succeed. Therefore, many of us seek out institutions with highly advanced educators. These are now known as colleges or universities. Although the Romans would seek out higher education at a much younger age, the system was the same as it is today. And both systems had the same two problems: Lack of accessibility for the entire society, and the overwhelming focus on knowledge-based teachings rather than creative or perspective-based teachings.

Accessibility of education is essential for a society to maintain a growing level of CSW. If education is not fully accessible, then only the families that can afford to get educated will continue to get educated. This will lead to an invisible oligarchy of a minority of the population controlling the entire society simply because most everybody else is not educated enough to know how to fight the system, or at times to even understand that there is an oligarchy at all.

The other issue with both Roman and modern western education systems, especially in the United States, is the almost total disregard for creative and perspective-based learning. American schools teach math, oratory skills, and literature analysis, but not how to create, discover, try new things, or attempt to understand what is not understood. Students are kept within a strict curriculum without any chance to innovate or be exposed to other perspectives outside of their communities. This is rather ironic considering the enormous desire for employers to find "innovators" or other people who can "think outside the box."

Furthermore, there must be education on why it is important to understand other individuals and cultures, and their perspectives and actions. This type of teaching is completely absent from American education, which again is ironic because the United States is filled with thousands of vastly different cultures and communities.

In fact, Mexico requires every student attending an institution of higher education to complete 480 hours of work in the social services before they graduate. This applies to students of every major. In 2012, the 780,000 Mexican students in higher education completed over 374 million hours of work in the social services (Cantón & Ramos, 2013). This type of program is exceptional for two reasons.

The first is that millions of hours of intelligent work are being completed to directly help those who are less fortunate. More importantly, these students are completing this work at a time where they are still developing their perspectives on the world. By being engrossed in work in the field of social services at a young age, these students will grow up always remembering those who may be disadvantaged.

The program also helps the college students better understand how social services programs work and how they can help, and furthermore, they can better understand what others are going through and what their needs may be. There is no better way to understand what a community is experiencing than to interact directly with them over an extended period of time and listen with open ears. Attempting to understand communities that are different from one's own is essential to maintaining healthy interconnectivity and thus increasing Collective Societal Wisdom.

The importance of interconnectivity leads us to the next solution: Opening our minds, borders, culture, ideas, and perspectives, to everybody – even those we do not understand.

Bringing people together allows for the exchange of different knowledge, ideas, perspectives, opinions, and experiences. As explained previously, integrating multiple ideas is how we innovate, create change, and ultimately progress. This must happen on a societal level.

The majority of the population within the United States generally has very low levels of global awareness and it seems that many do not wish to change that. If you talk to most Americans about what is going on in the rest of the world, I would guess that the majority of them do not know and many may not even care. Some may have heard the latest news headlines but that is most likely the extent of their knowledge.

This type of individualistic attitude not only affects how the US acts regarding other nations but how communities within the US act towards each other. As we know, misunderstanding one another or any sort of actor that may be unknown or misunderstood by another community can lead to fear. Fear leads to tensions, and many times, violence.

The 2019 Global Peace Index (GPI), which takes into account both foreign and domestic violence from a single nation, as well as other factors such as ease of access to purchase firearms, ranked the United States at 128 out of 163 countries with 1 being the most peaceful and 163 being the most violent (Institute for Economics & Peace, 2019).

In other words, the United States ranks in the bottom quarter, or most violent quarter, of 163 countries regarding its attitudes on violence concerning both internal and external conflicts. Sadly, the US has seen a 19-rank deterioration in only two years from its rank at 109 in 2016. Currently, the US ranks in the same GPI quarter percentile as Syria, Afghanistan, North Korea, Russia, and Iraq - nations that many Americans would consider extremely violent.

Another interesting finding from the GPI 2019 report is that "As peacefulness increases, so does satisfaction with life, freedom, and feelings of respect" (Institute for Economics & Peace, 2019).

With the exception of the United States, that is. The US has some of the highest ratings of perceived "freedom of life" and "standard of living satisfaction" ratings amongst its populace, notwithstanding being in the bottom quarter of peacefulness on a global scale.

This certainly says something about the American people. Despite being a violent nation compared to other nations globally, most Americans are either completely unaware of this fact, or do not seem to care. Or maybe some believe that violence between people is inevitable and cannot be helped. Any one of these explanations will have severe long-term effects on the US, and these effects can already be seen. Further along in the report, the GPI explains that North America is the only region in the world to suffer a decline in feelings of "freedom of life" and "standard of living satisfaction" over the last ten years (Institute for Economics & Peace, 2019).

This cannot continue. There must be a new program integrated into the public education system that allows people to understand each other and experience what they may not normally experience in their own environment. I hope with all my heart that all you who are more intelligent and creative than I am can figure out a solution that addresses these concerns, but for now, this is what I have come up with:

Direct human contact is the only effective way to exchange knowledge and perspectives in order to improve Collective Societal Wisdom. Therefore, there must be a way to provide contact between various communities of students in their general education. Hence, I suggest providing a rotation system, in which students spend some time, it does not have to be long, in various communities that reside in quite different environments. Just as high school students rotate classes to provide different types of learning, students should rotate communities (or even countries) to provide different types of perspectives.

Since this type of system will most likely be quite slow to plan, secure funding, and implement, we can use the same ideas to create a class that could be integrated into the current classroom-based education system. Although this will not be effective as students actually being immersed in other various cultures and communities, it would still be much better than the current education where there is little to no contact with anyone from outside communities.

The class that should be implemented would be designed exclusively to provide students the opportunities to interact and learn about different cultures while also teaching other communities about his or her own community.

For example, say we implement this class into 10th grade. Most sophomores in high school are old enough to know social skills and can show respect but are still sensitive to the needs of others. In other words, they are still young in the sense that they are not set in their ways yet and are still building their values and identity.

The 10th graders in this class would put together a presentation about the people within their classroom including their opinions on various issues and the reasoning behind it, their struggles or daily stressors, the wonderful things about their community, what they do in their free time for fun, and even what their family life is like. Essentially, these students will compile a presentation based on what their community looks like, what makes their community great, and what is difficult about living in that community.

Then, other classrooms from schools in different types of communities will come to their school to visit their community. The students will present whatever they have come up with to these visiting schools to inform them about their own community and social values. Another part of the day could be showing the visitors around their community to give the opportunity for the students to build friendships, exchange contact info, and hopefully stay in touch over the long term. Likewise, when this classroom is not presenting, they will go around and listen to the presentations of other communities over the course of the school year.

Thus, each class of 10th graders will be presenting about themselves, since they know themselves best, while also rotating through various types of communities to learn from the people who actually are a part of those communities. If this is implemented on a national scale, this type of program will build understanding between people of different backgrounds and forge a greater level of interconnectivity on a societal level. In fact, this program could even be implemented internationally so that students may travel around to various nations and be immersed in different cultures.

Some may be wondering what are the different "types" of communities I am referring to. A useful way to organize this would be to ensure each school must present to, and hear the presentation from, a school which is in a community with lower socioeconomic status and a community which is more affluent than the school in question. Furthermore, there should include communities that are largely made up of immigrants, for example Chinatown, or a community that is mostly Latino, or Little Italy. There should also be religious communities included in this, for example, a Muslim community or a Mormon community. Exchanging presentations with a refugee community would be eye-opening as well.

Of course, it may even be more interesting to ask the students what types of communities they would want to learn from. They will almost certainly be more creative than what us adults can come up with.

Overall, there must be a specific time devoted to building human connections outside of one's own community in the public school system. Usually the only time Americans have a chance at interacting with people from various backgrounds is if they attend a large university. However, many people at universities end up spending most of their time with those who have similar backgrounds and end up learning very little about other communities anyway. Furthermore, the rest of the population who does not attend a large, diverse university, or college at all, may not have any chance to interact with people from different communities or backgrounds.

Most people hang out with those from similar backgrounds and end up working with those in similar backgrounds. This is why it is essential for various communities to be given opportunities to interact with each other. If it is not included in the basic education system, most people will not go out of their way to interact with and learn from people different than themselves.

In addition to the need for a program that builds interconnectivity among the future generations, there must be a revival of support for innovation and the creative arts. Creativity equals innovation. Innovation begets progress. Rather than shutting down the creative outlets for individuals, we should be encouraging every individual to utilize some sort of creative outlet to continue building that part of their brain.

The idea that we should only focus on building skills that we will use for "work" is inherently flawed. In fact, by having a strong creative outlet that is allowed to flourish, we will almost certainly be more creative at work as well. This could translate to finding more profitable ways of doing business, better marketing, discovering new technology, or any sort of idea that can improve some aspect of that field of work or study.

Hence, children, adolescents, and even adults, should not only be encouraged to find enjoyable creative outlets, but these opportunities should be made abundant. In the Western world, there is a perceived duality between creatives and capitalists, or in other words, artists and businesspeople. However, many individuals have skills in both areas. Because of the performance-based nature of the Western world, particularly the United States, it is deemed better to only focus on work skills and completely disregard the creative arts. Unfortunately, human beings do not function in dualities. And I would argue that those who are constantly using all parts of their brains rather than only one will be more productive at work, have better lives at home, and be more successful and happier in general.

Many successful and happy people have a number of hobbies they like to do outside of work. So why are children discouraged if their hobbies happen to be art or music?

Both the interconnectivity program and the increase in creative arts within the lives of individuals, especially young people, could, and should be implemented into the general education system. Of course, the central argument that many individuals use as to why education cannot be improved or expanded, is cost. Cost is also the reason that countless people use to explain why education should not be made more accessible to a wider range of people.

Let's consider this argument that expanding accessibility and quality of education "costs too much."

First, let's discuss the economic implications of making all education, even advanced education such as college, free for anybody. As we know, college tuition costs in the United States have skyrocketed over the last few decades. This issue alone has had drastic effects on the overall economy.

In fact, the issues have been so widespread that the Federal Reserve released a report in January 2019 outlining their own research and opinions on the effects of student loan debt on Americans between the ages of 24 and 32 buying homes. The

Federal Reserve found that from 2005 to 2014, student loans prevented an estimated 400,000 individuals between the ages of 24 and 32 from purchasing a home. The study further found that higher student loan debt greatly increases the likelihood of these individuals defaulting on their loans later in life, thus negatively impacting their credit scores. Low credit scores then prevent these individuals from securing other loans for homes or cars, or in other words, putting money back into the greater economy (Board of Governors of the Federal Reserve System, 2019).

In 2017, a report published by the National Association of Realtors in conjunction with the American Student Assistance agency discovered that student loan debt alone is delaying the purchase of homes of millennials by a median of seven years based on a survey of 92,000 student loan borrowers (National Association of REALTORS® Research Department And American Student Assistance®, 2017). This means that for seven years, there is a lack of real money entering back into the economy from these young people. For obvious reasons, this can hugely affect the economy.

The average American lives an average of about 80 years. Say the average American starts working at 16 and retires at 65, making his or her economic lifespan, the time during which he or she is making money and cycling it back into the economy by buying things, is around 49 years.

Knowing that the average student loan borrower is prevented from making any significant purchase such as a house for seven years, we can conclude that student loans are eliminating 7/49 years, or 1/7, of this person's economic lifespan where they could be paying mortgages, property taxes, or upgrading their home. But instead, they are paying back their student loans.

We know from the Fed's report that this accounts for at least 400,000 individuals. But imagine if education was made free, or very low-cost. That would allow these 400,000+ individuals to purchase houses, cars, or anything they want. Think of the future generations as well. If every college student could purchase a house right out of college, the housing market would take off. The current student loan debt is over $1.5 trillion, but imagine if that $1.5 trillion could be cycled into the direct economy in the form of mortgages or other consumer loans, rather than loans to pay for-profit universities.

Thus, the argument that the "cost" of increasing accessibility for education would be too great does not take into account the opportunity cost of essentially stifling the younger generations' spending capabilities in the mainstream economy. In other words, promoting increased educational opportunities for a greater proportion of the population will generate more economic growth by allowing those people to get better jobs, pay more into social security, and put more money into the economy through their increased purchasing power, including the capacity to buy homes. In short, the issue of college tuition costs is a battle between short-term and long-term costs.

There is also the argument surrounding quality of education. I already discussed the importance of the creative arts and innovation. However, imagine if everybody was educated about personal finance and investment opportunities. For instance, lower-income families usually do not have many sound investments because they either do not know how to invest, or do not have enough extra money to afford to put away money on the side. The minimum wage issue is an additional issue that an entire book could be written about but let's focus on financial education. Also, if people understand the benefits, they might be able to find some extra dollars that they could invest, instead of some of the discretionary spending that we all fall victim to such as buying the new PlayStation or getting our nails done.

Imagine if lower-income families were educated about the stock market, or IRA's, for example. Despite what some conservatives might think, this would actually be profitable for them as well. If everybody was educated on how to invest in stocks, for instance, the millions of people who do not invest currently might start putting money into the stock market. A massive influx of new money into the market would make everybody wealthier, including those who have lower incomes.

Increasing the accessibility and quality of education is not only crucial for societal progress but is also profitable. We must all work to educate others on these issues and take action to spark the changes needed.

The solutions described above are only a small portion of the changes that needs to be implemented in the United States today, however, as I have stated many times, I hope that every reader of this book will spread their knowledge, expertise, perspectives, and experiences to those around them and those far away so that we can collectively bring the world out of this funk and onto a new path of progress.

There is one more important issue that must be discussed. I understand that countless people around the world know that the world is at risk for societal regression. However, do not lose hope. Humans are the most powerful species in the world because of our ability to adapt and stimulate the changes that we need. Despite what many may think, entire societies can make massive change relatively quickly with the right knowledge provided.

Jared Diamond's most recent book, *Upheaval*[11] (See Further Readings), explains how six countries overcame significant upheavals and instead entered new ages of great success. The same can be done in the United States. However, we must learn from our own past mistakes as well as others, and be open to all kinds of solutions, some which may require some painful responsibility for current and past wrongdoing.

I have great hope for the future but we still must constantly remind each other that we do have the capacity for macro-level change, we must simply unite and stop at nothing to achieve the ultimate goal, to increase the well-being of the future generations for all people and all communities.

Final Thoughts

I congratulate you on making it this far in the book, despite the wide variety of issues discussed. I truly thank you for taking the interest and time in my thoughts. I hope that every reader will spread the word about the dangers of a fear-based society and will work together to find and implement solutions for the various issues in our societal system and global network.

Always remember: Non-action is a policy. Indecision is a decision.

Make face-to-face human connections with as many people as you can. Educate those around you. Take advantage of your rights and speak, act, vote, do whatever you need to do to activate the changes you want to see in the world.

My solutions presented are incredibly broad and are only one man's ideas for change. I hope that all of you who are much more intelligent and experienced than I am can work together to create stronger, more detailed solutions than what I could ever come up with. And of course, if you do, I should hope that you take the idea and run with it and stop at nothing until it becomes a reality.

Furthermore, for those of you who are research-oriented, you can help too. Discover the true meanings behind the various interrelated issues discussed in this book. Find out how we can use theories like Collective Societal Wisdom or the Tragedy of Isolated Perspective to implement strategies that will make the world stronger, healthier, and more peaceful.

My hope is that this book can reach anybody who truly wishes to improve his or her society so that those who have less opportunity can be educated and do everything in their power to strive for change.

Only widespread cooperation and a single, shared vision of a unified world can steer the world away from the next Dark Ages and bring humanity into a new era of unprecedented interconnectivity, understanding, care, love, and peace.

Further Readings

[1]Views on humanity in the modern world and the collapse or success of societal institutions in the present and the past:

> Costa, R. D. (2010). *The Watchman's Rattle.* Philadelphia, PA: Vanguard Press.

> Eisenstein, C. (2007). *The Ascent of Humanity.* Berkeley, CA: Evolver Editions.

> Harari, Y. N. (2015). *Sapiens.* New York, NY: HarperCollins.

> Kolbert, E. (2014). *The Sixth Extinction.* Henry Holt and Company.

[2]On the history of social welfare policy in the United States:

Karger, H. J., & Stoesz, D. (2014). *American Social Welfare Policy: A Pluralist Approach* (Seventh ed.). Upper Saddle River, NJ: Pearson Education Inc.

[3]On macroeconomics in the United States and monetary policy trends for the future:

Summers, G. (2017). *The Everything Bubble.* Graham Summers.

[4]On habitual decision-making and habit loops:

Duhigg, C. (2012). Power of Habit: Why We Do What We Do in Life and Business. New York, NY: Random House.

[5]On the Roman Empire and its similarities to the United States:

Aldrete, G. S. (2008). *Daily Life in the Roman City.* University of Oklahoma Press.

Parkin, T. G., & Pomeroy, A. J. (2007). *Roman Social History.* London and New York: Routledge.

[6]On the connections within the brain in excruciating detail:

> Kennedy, H., Van Essen, D. C., & Christen, Y. (2016). *Micro-, Meso- and Macro-Connectomics of the Brain.* Springer International Publishing AG Switzerland.

[7]On Dunbar's number explaining the cognitive limit on social relationships:

> Dunbar, R. I. (1992). Neocortex size as a constraint on group size in primates. Journal of Human Evolution, 469-493.

[8]Critiques on medication and the current perceptions and solutions surrounding mental health:

> Frances, A. (2013). *Essentials of Psychiatric Diagnosis.* New York, NY: The Guilford Press.

> Hari, J. (2018). *Lost Connections.* New York, NY: Bloomsbury USA.

[9]On the power of exercise on the brain:

> Ratey, J. J. (2008). Spark: The Revolutionary New Science of Exercise and the Brain. Little, Brown Spark.

[10]On early Christianity and its various historical internal and external conflicts:

Lynch, J. H. (2010). *Early Christianity.* New York, NY: Oxford University Press.

[11]On the incredible triumphs over hardship by entire societies:

Diamond, J. (2019). Upheaval. New York, NY: Little, Brown and Company.

References

Aldrete, G. S. (2008). *Daily Life in the Roman City.* University of Oklahoma Press.

Amazon Now Has Nearly 50% of US Ecommerce Market. (2018, July 16). Retrieved from eMarketer.

Avert. (2019, February 26). *HIV and AIDS in East and Souhtern Africa Regional Overview.* Retrieved from Avert.

Baldwin, L. V. (1986). Malcolm X and Martin Luther King Jr.: What They Thought About Each Other. *Islamic Studies*, 395-416.

Beard, M. (Writer), & MacGregor, H. (Director). (2012). *Meet the Romans* [Motion Picture]. BBC.

Board of Governors of the Federal Reserve System. (2019). *Consumer & Community Context Vol.1 No. 1.* Board of Governors of the Federal Reserve System.

Brown, M. (2018, April 3). *What Would You Do For A Raise? | 35% of Americans Would Give Up the Right to Vote.* Retrieved from LEND EDU.

Cantón, A., & Ramos, E. (2013). *Mandating Service: Mexico's National Requirement.* Retrieved from Association of American Colleges & Universities.

https://www.aacu.org/diversitydemocracy/2013/
fall/canton-ramos

Costa, R. D. (2010). *The Watchman's Rattle.*
Philadelphia, PA: Vanguard Press.

Diamond, J. (2019). *Upheaval.* New York, NY: Little,
Brown and Company.

Downie, R. (2016, Febraury 27). *The 5 Best-Performing
Stocks in the Past 20 Years.* Retrieved from
Investopedia.

Duhigg, C. (2012). *Power of Habit: Why We Do What
We Do in Life and Business.* New York, NY:
Random House.

Dunbar, R. I. (1992). Neocortex size as a constraint on
group size in primates. *Journal of Human
Evolution,* 469-493.

Eisenstein, C. (2007). *The Ascent of Humanity.*
Berkeley, CA: Evolver Editions.

Elliot, C. P. (2014). The Acceptance and Value of
Roman Silver Coinage in the Second and Third
Centuries AD. *The Numismatic Chronicle, 174,*
129-152.

Epictetus. (1994). *The Art of Living.* (S. Lebell, Trans.)
New York, NY: HarperCollins.

Frances, A. (2013). *Essentials of Psychiatric Diagnosis.*
New York, NY: The Guilford Press.

Haque, U. (2018, April 6). *Why The World is Ripping Itself Apart: Five Ways History's Repeating Itself.* Retrieved from Eudaimonia & Co.

Harari, Y. N. (2015). *Sapiens.* New York, NY: HarperCollins.

Hari, J. (2018). *Lost Connections.* New York, NY: Bloomsbury USA.

Institute for Economics & Peace. (2019). *Global Peace Index 2019.* Sydney, Australia: Institute for Economics & Peace.

Jones, T. (2016, April). *Technology & Patent Research.* Retrieved from China vs. U.S. Patent Trends. How Do the Giants Stack Up?.

Keating, E. (2015, December 3). *The 20 most used business buzzwords of 2015.* Retrieved from Smartcompany.

Kennedy, H., Van Essen, D. C., & Christen, Y. (2016). Form Meets Function in the Brain: Observing the Activity and Structure of Specific Neural Connections. In *Micro-, Meso- and Macro-Connectomics of the Brain.* Springer International Publishing AG Switzerland.

Kolbert, E. (2014). *The Sixth Extinction.* Henry Holt and Company.

López, G., Bialik, K., & Radford, J. (2018, November 30). *Key findings about U.S. immigrants.* Retrieved from Pew Research Center.

Lynch, J. H. (2010). *Early Christianity.* New York, NY: Oxford University Press.

Marcellinus, A. (n.d.). The Roman History of Ammianus Marcellinus: Liber XXXI. In *The Roman History of Ammianus Marcellinus* (B. Thayer, Trans.). Loeb Classical Library.

Mommsen, T. (1996). *A History of Rome under the Emperors.* (T. Wiedemann, Ed., & C. Krojzl, Trans.) London and New York: Routledge.

National Association of REALTORS® Research Department And American Student Assistance®. (2017). *Student Loan Debt and Housing Report 2017.* National Association of REALTORS® Research Department And American Student Assistance®.

National Center for Education Statistics. (2012). *The Nation's Report Card: 2011.* Washington, D.C.: Institute of Education Sciences, US Department of Education.

New American Standard New Testament Greek Lexicon. (n.d.). *Ekklesia.*

OECD. (2017). *OECD Health Statistics: Health care resources.* Organisation for Economic Co-operation and Development.

Parkin, T. G., & Pomeroy, A. J. (2007). *Roman Social History.* London and New York: Routledge.

Poushter, J., Fetterolf, J., & Tamir, C. (2019). *A Changing World: Global Views on Diversity,*

*Gender Equality, Family Life and the
Importance of Religion.* Pew Research Center.

Ratey, J. J. (2008). *Spark: The Revolutionary New
Science of Exercise and the Brain.* Little, Brown
Spark.

(2019). *Steel Imports Report: United States.*
Washington, D.C.: International Trade
Administration.

Summers, G. (2017). *The Everything Bubble.* Graham
Summers.

United States Census Bureau. (2018). *QuickFacts United
States.* Washington, D.C.: US Department of
Commerce.

United States of America Trade Profile. (n.d.). Retrieved
from World Trade Organization.

WTO Statistics Database. (n.d.). Retrieved from World
Trade Organization.

Acknowledgements

I acknowledge with great joy and gratitude my family, friends, colleagues, and mentors, without whom this project would have not been possible.

I first recognize my brother Luke for always supporting me in my endeavors and helping narrow down my broad ideas into presentable arguments.

My parents, Naomi and Ron, were always sources of encouragement and assistance throughout my life, and especially in this project. I credit Naomi with the idea to compile the above information into a book.

I am grateful for my grandmother Nora, who edited just about every aspect of the manuscript, sent me numerous articles, books, and other references, and constantly inspired me to continue grinding through the arduous process of creating a book.

My close friend and colleague, Samantha, designed the book cover and has provided words of encouragement and support regarding the project since its inception.

I acknowledge all my professors of classics, history, political analysis, and psychology at the University of Iowa for providing me with the understanding of current and past societal systems, which changed the way I see the world and its people. I also thank my professors of social work at Loyola University Chicago for giving me the information needed to observe and analyze how the environment of an individual or group directly impacts their actions and mindsets.

Finally, I wish to show my gratitude for all my friends, classmates, colleagues, and mentors who helped provide their knowledge, insights, and perspectives on the topics covered in this project, which ultimately helped inform my perspectives and ideas presented in this book.

To all those who were a direct part of this project, and to those who were in my life as indirect supports for the duration of this project, I express my deepest thanks.

About the Author

Max Parrella has extensively studied classical history, American history, political analysis, psychology, clinical social work, and social policy. Max received his B.A. in Ancient Civilizations from the University of Iowa and is currently completing his Master's in Social Work at Loyola University Chicago.

His background in ancient civilizations, political analysis, and social work gives Max a unique perspective on the various political and social events that have occurred on a global scale, many of which have caused distress to numerous communities.

By combining his knowledge of both macro-level systems and clinical social work, complemented by psychological theory, Max has the ability to understand how the minds of individuals can impact entire societies and how social environments and policies can impact the individual.

Max has attempted to reign in this knowledge and present it in an understandable way in his new book, *Collective Societal Wisdom: The Centerpiece to the Longevity of Civilization.*

Get in touch with Max Parrella

www.maxparrella.com

CPSIA information can be obtained
at www.ICGtesting.com
Printed in the USA
LVHW042026281019
635535LV00001B/31

9 781734 111118